SPECTRUM®

Math

Grade 3

Published by Spectrum®
an imprint of Carson-Dellosa Publishing LLC
Greensboro, NC

Spectrum®
An imprint of Carson-Dellosa Publishing LLC
PO Box 35665
Greensboro, NC 27425 USA

ISBN 978-1-4838-0871-0

03-098197784

Table of Contents Grade 3

Table of Contents, continued

Check What You Know

Adding and Subtracting 1- and 2-Digit Numbers (with renaming)

Add.

	a	b	c	d	e
1.	23 +19	17 + 5	37 +42	11 +75	81 + 9
2.	16 + 3	83 +11	43 +14	22 +59	64 + 6
3.	30 +23	7 +25	9 +36	18 +25	93 + 2
4.	13 +86	75 3 +16	13 33 + 7	40 51 + 2	15 27 +46

Subtract.

	a	b	c	d	e
5.	90 −10	16 − 9	23 −18	27 − 7	19 −11
6.	57 −16	84 −23	16 −11	25 − 5	62 −19
7.	97 −58	46 −23	81 −27	48 −13	74 − 9
8.	32 −24	73 −12	65 −30	70 −20	23 − 8

Check What You Know

Adding and Subtracting 1- and 2-Digit Numbers (with renaming)

Solve each problem.

9. The florist has 63 roses and carnations. If she has 27 roses, how many carnations does she have?

The florist has _____ roses and carnations.

She has _____ roses.

The florist has _____ carnations.

9.

10. Bly has 43 pennies, 13 dimes, and 16 nickels. How many coins does she have in all?

Bly has _____ pennies.

She has _____ dimes.

She has _____ nickels.

Bly has _____ coins in all.

10.

11. There are 36 students in Cleveland's class this year. If 22 are girls, how many boys are in Cleveland's class?

There are _____ students in Cleveland's class.

There are _____ girls in his class.

There are _____ boys in his class.

11.

12. The store has 53 cases of apples and oranges in the storeroom. If there are 28 cases of apples, how many cases of oranges are there in the storeroom?

There are _____ cases of oranges in the storeroom.

12.

Lesson 1.1 Adding through 20

addend   3 ⟶ Find the **3**-row.
addend   + 8 ⟶ Find the **8**-column.
sum   1 1 ⟵ The sum is named
where the 3-row and
the 8-column meet.

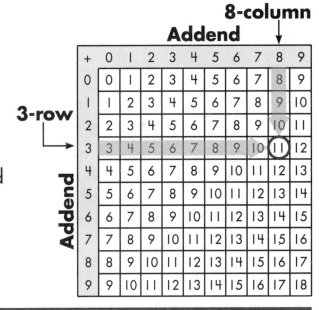

Add.

	a	b	c	d	e	f
1.	2 +3 5	7 +9	2 +5	1 +7	0 +3	9 +5
2.	7 +2	3 +3	9 +0	6 +5	0 +7	8 +5
3.	4 +3	2 +9	7 +7	5 +6	5 +9	0 +6
4.	0 +0	8 +3	8 +6	6 +1	5 +3	4 +8
5.	5 +2	3 +1	2 +4	8 +2	8 +8	3 +6
6.	0 +9	5 +7	3 +9	6 +9	9 +9	5 +7

Lesson 1.2 Subtracting through 20

7-column

–	0	1	2	3	4	5	6	7	8	9
0	0	1	2	3	4	5	6	7	8	9
1	1	2	3	4	5	6	7	8	9	10
2	2	3	4	5	6	7	8	9	10	11
3	3	4	5	6	7	8	9	10	11	12
4	4	5	6	7	8	9	10	11	12	13
5	5	6	7	8	9	10	11	12	13	14
6	6	7	8	9	10	11	12	13	14	15
7	7	8	9	10	11	12	13	14	15	16
8	8	9	10	11	12	13	14	15	16	17
9	9	10	11	12	13	14	15	16	17	18

minuend   1 2 → Find the **12** in
subtrahend   – 7 → the **7**-column.
difference   5 ← The difference is the number at the end of the row.

Subtract.

	a	b	c	d	e	f
1.	$\begin{array}{r} 7 \\ -2 \\ \hline 5 \end{array}$	$\begin{array}{r} 6 \\ -0 \\ \hline \end{array}$	$\begin{array}{r} 5 \\ -4 \\ \hline \end{array}$	$\begin{array}{r} 11 \\ -\ 6 \\ \hline \end{array}$	$\begin{array}{r} 16 \\ -\ 9 \\ \hline \end{array}$	$\begin{array}{r} 13 \\ -\ 8 \\ \hline \end{array}$
2.	$\begin{array}{r} 6 \\ -3 \\ \hline \end{array}$	$\begin{array}{r} 9 \\ -6 \\ \hline \end{array}$	$\begin{array}{r} 5 \\ -2 \\ \hline \end{array}$	$\begin{array}{r} 8 \\ -0 \\ \hline \end{array}$	$\begin{array}{r} 18 \\ -\ 9 \\ \hline \end{array}$	$\begin{array}{r} 9 \\ -7 \\ \hline \end{array}$
3.	$\begin{array}{r} 7 \\ -2 \\ \hline \end{array}$	$\begin{array}{r} 3 \\ -0 \\ \hline \end{array}$	$\begin{array}{r} 8 \\ -2 \\ \hline \end{array}$	$\begin{array}{r} 7 \\ -4 \\ \hline \end{array}$	$\begin{array}{r} 10 \\ -\ 3 \\ \hline \end{array}$	$\begin{array}{r} 9 \\ -2 \\ \hline \end{array}$
4.	$\begin{array}{r} 14 \\ -\ 3 \\ \hline \end{array}$	$\begin{array}{r} 3 \\ -2 \\ \hline \end{array}$	$\begin{array}{r} 14 \\ -\ 6 \\ \hline \end{array}$	$\begin{array}{r} 13 \\ -\ 5 \\ \hline \end{array}$	$\begin{array}{r} 13 \\ -\ 8 \\ \hline \end{array}$	$\begin{array}{r} 17 \\ -\ 4 \\ \hline \end{array}$
5.	$\begin{array}{r} 12 \\ -\ 5 \\ \hline \end{array}$	$\begin{array}{r} 6 \\ -4 \\ \hline \end{array}$	$\begin{array}{r} 1 \\ -0 \\ \hline \end{array}$	$\begin{array}{r} 12 \\ -\ 3 \\ \hline \end{array}$	$\begin{array}{r} 10 \\ -\ 6 \\ \hline \end{array}$	$\begin{array}{r} 11 \\ -\ 5 \\ \hline \end{array}$
6.	$\begin{array}{r} 3 \\ -1 \\ \hline \end{array}$	$\begin{array}{r} 15 \\ -\ 9 \\ \hline \end{array}$	$\begin{array}{r} 9 \\ -1 \\ \hline \end{array}$	$\begin{array}{r} 5 \\ -1 \\ \hline \end{array}$	$\begin{array}{r} 8 \\ -7 \\ \hline \end{array}$	$\begin{array}{r} 14 \\ -\ 8 \\ \hline \end{array}$

Lesson 1.3 Adding 2-Digit Numbers (no renaming)

First, add the ones.   Then, add the tens.

$$
\begin{array}{r} 43 \\ +22 \\ \hline \end{array}
\qquad
\begin{array}{r} 43 \\ +22 \\ \hline 5 \end{array}
\qquad
\begin{array}{r} 43 \\ +22 \\ \hline 65 \end{array}
\quad
\begin{array}{l} \text{addend} \\ \text{addend} \\ \\ \text{sum} \end{array}
$$

$$
\begin{array}{r} 22 \\ +16 \\ \hline 38 \end{array}
\quad
\begin{array}{l} \text{addend} \\ \text{addend} \\ \\ \text{sum} \end{array}
$$

- - - First, add the ones.
- - - Then, add the tens.

Add.

	a	b	c	d	e	f
1.	23 +16 **39**	11 +22	20 +10	16 +12	73 +15	63 +13
2.	10 +17	18 +30	13 +14	32 +51	81 +11	34 +21
3.	14 +12	34 +13	41 +18	30 +50	27 +50	22 +22
4.	18 +41	13 +42	12 +44	31 +17	27 +42	31 +38
5.	13 +14	15 +43	23 +42	22 +71	37 +60	35 +23
6.	10 +43	73 +20	86 +13	52 +13	42 +26	32 +45

Lesson 1.4 Subtracting 2-Digit Numbers (no renaming)

First, subtract the ones.   Then, subtract the tens.

$$
\begin{array}{r} 36 \\ -23 \\ \hline \end{array}
\qquad
\begin{array}{r} 36 \\ -23 \\ \hline 3 \end{array}
\qquad
\begin{array}{r} 36 \\ -23 \\ \hline 13 \end{array}
\qquad
\begin{array}{l} \text{minuend} \\ \text{subtrahend} \\[4pt] \text{difference} \end{array}
$$

Subtract.

	a	b	c	d	e	f
1.	$\begin{array}{r}23\\-12\\\hline 11\end{array}$	$\begin{array}{r}86\\-22\\\hline\end{array}$	$\begin{array}{r}93\\-71\\\hline\end{array}$	$\begin{array}{r}30\\-10\\\hline\end{array}$	$\begin{array}{r}92\\-11\\\hline\end{array}$	$\begin{array}{r}48\\-16\\\hline\end{array}$
2.	$\begin{array}{r}62\\-10\\\hline\end{array}$	$\begin{array}{r}83\\-13\\\hline\end{array}$	$\begin{array}{r}65\\-44\\\hline\end{array}$	$\begin{array}{r}54\\-12\\\hline\end{array}$	$\begin{array}{r}37\\-25\\\hline\end{array}$	$\begin{array}{r}88\\-32\\\hline\end{array}$
3.	$\begin{array}{r}86\\-45\\\hline\end{array}$	$\begin{array}{r}92\\-70\\\hline\end{array}$	$\begin{array}{r}89\\-62\\\hline\end{array}$	$\begin{array}{r}75\\-62\\\hline\end{array}$	$\begin{array}{r}88\\-44\\\hline\end{array}$	$\begin{array}{r}90\\-60\\\hline\end{array}$
4.	$\begin{array}{r}82\\-41\\\hline\end{array}$	$\begin{array}{r}57\\-36\\\hline\end{array}$	$\begin{array}{r}35\\-23\\\hline\end{array}$	$\begin{array}{r}65\\-43\\\hline\end{array}$	$\begin{array}{r}81\\-60\\\hline\end{array}$	$\begin{array}{r}42\\-30\\\hline\end{array}$
5.	$\begin{array}{r}60\\-30\\\hline\end{array}$	$\begin{array}{r}46\\-25\\\hline\end{array}$	$\begin{array}{r}92\\-81\\\hline\end{array}$	$\begin{array}{r}86\\-32\\\hline\end{array}$	$\begin{array}{r}57\\-36\\\hline\end{array}$	$\begin{array}{r}29\\-13\\\hline\end{array}$
6.	$\begin{array}{r}25\\-15\\\hline\end{array}$	$\begin{array}{r}28\\-12\\\hline\end{array}$	$\begin{array}{r}36\\-13\\\hline\end{array}$	$\begin{array}{r}46\\-15\\\hline\end{array}$	$\begin{array}{r}75\\-14\\\hline\end{array}$	$\begin{array}{r}64\\-23\\\hline\end{array}$

Lesson 1.5 Adding 2-Digit Numbers (with renaming)

Add the ones.   Add the tens.
Rename 12 as 10 + 2.

$$
\begin{array}{r} 37 \\ +25 \\ \hline \end{array}
\qquad
\begin{array}{r} 7 \\ +\ 5 \\ \hline 12 \end{array} \text{ or } 10 + 2
\qquad
\begin{array}{r} {}^{1}\ \\ 37 \\ +25 \\ \hline 2 \end{array}
\qquad
\begin{array}{r} {}^{1}\ \\ 37 \\ +25 \\ \hline 62 \end{array}
\quad
\begin{array}{l} \text{addend} \\ \text{addend} \\ \\ \text{sum} \end{array}
$$

Add.

	a	b	c	d	e	f
1.	$\begin{array}{r}23\\+18\\\hline 41\end{array}$	$\begin{array}{r}76\\+15\\\hline\end{array}$	$\begin{array}{r}13\\+77\\\hline\end{array}$	$\begin{array}{r}36\\+16\\\hline\end{array}$	$\begin{array}{r}19\\+62\\\hline\end{array}$	$\begin{array}{r}29\\+19\\\hline\end{array}$
2.	$\begin{array}{r}27\\+36\\\hline\end{array}$	$\begin{array}{r}52\\+39\\\hline\end{array}$	$\begin{array}{r}36\\+28\\\hline\end{array}$	$\begin{array}{r}30\\+50\\\hline\end{array}$	$\begin{array}{r}56\\+27\\\hline\end{array}$	$\begin{array}{r}59\\+13\\\hline\end{array}$
3.	$\begin{array}{r}54\\+27\\\hline\end{array}$	$\begin{array}{r}53\\+28\\\hline\end{array}$	$\begin{array}{r}28\\+17\\\hline\end{array}$	$\begin{array}{r}13\\+19\\\hline\end{array}$	$\begin{array}{r}39\\+17\\\hline\end{array}$	$\begin{array}{r}56\\+14\\\hline\end{array}$
4.	$\begin{array}{r}62\\+19\\\hline\end{array}$	$\begin{array}{r}27\\+18\\\hline\end{array}$	$\begin{array}{r}26\\+55\\\hline\end{array}$	$\begin{array}{r}18\\+13\\\hline\end{array}$	$\begin{array}{r}72\\+18\\\hline\end{array}$	$\begin{array}{r}37\\+17\\\hline\end{array}$
5.	$\begin{array}{r}23\\+57\\\hline\end{array}$	$\begin{array}{r}29\\+16\\\hline\end{array}$	$\begin{array}{r}25\\+16\\\hline\end{array}$	$\begin{array}{r}38\\+14\\\hline\end{array}$	$\begin{array}{r}26\\+28\\\hline\end{array}$	$\begin{array}{r}76\\+15\\\hline\end{array}$
6.	$\begin{array}{r}29\\+17\\\hline\end{array}$	$\begin{array}{r}34\\+27\\\hline\end{array}$	$\begin{array}{r}43\\+27\\\hline\end{array}$	$\begin{array}{r}25\\+26\\\hline\end{array}$	$\begin{array}{r}48\\+12\\\hline\end{array}$	$\begin{array}{r}45\\+46\\\hline\end{array}$

Lesson 1.6 Subtracting 2-Digit Numbers (with renaming)

Subtract the ones. Rename 52 as "4 tens and 12 ones."	Subtract the ones.	Subtract the tens.	
$\begin{array}{r} 52 \\ -19 \\ \hline \end{array}$	$\begin{array}{r} {}^{4}\,{}^{12} \\ \cancel{5}\cancel{2} \\ -19 \\ \hline \end{array}$	$\begin{array}{r} {}^{4}\,{}^{12} \\ \cancel{5}\cancel{2} \\ -19 \\ \hline 3 \end{array}$	$\begin{array}{r} {}^{4}\,{}^{12} \\ \cancel{5}\cancel{2} \\ -19 \\ \hline 33 \end{array}$ minuend subtrahend difference

---

Subtract.

	a	**b**	**c**	**d**	**e**	**f**
1.	$\begin{array}{r} 30 \\ -22 \\ \hline 8 \end{array}$	$\begin{array}{r} 22 \\ -19 \\ \hline \end{array}$	$\begin{array}{r} 53 \\ -28 \\ \hline \end{array}$	$\begin{array}{r} 41 \\ -27 \\ \hline \end{array}$	$\begin{array}{r} 92 \\ -56 \\ \hline \end{array}$	$\begin{array}{r} 86 \\ -27 \\ \hline \end{array}$
2.	$\begin{array}{r} 83 \\ -66 \\ \hline \end{array}$	$\begin{array}{r} 62 \\ -56 \\ \hline \end{array}$	$\begin{array}{r} 51 \\ -17 \\ \hline \end{array}$	$\begin{array}{r} 34 \\ -15 \\ \hline \end{array}$	$\begin{array}{r} 46 \\ -29 \\ \hline \end{array}$	$\begin{array}{r} 57 \\ -38 \\ \hline \end{array}$
3.	$\begin{array}{r} 72 \\ -37 \\ \hline \end{array}$	$\begin{array}{r} 82 \\ -67 \\ \hline \end{array}$	$\begin{array}{r} 64 \\ -18 \\ \hline \end{array}$	$\begin{array}{r} 86 \\ -57 \\ \hline \end{array}$	$\begin{array}{r} 41 \\ -16 \\ \hline \end{array}$	$\begin{array}{r} 53 \\ -29 \\ \hline \end{array}$
4.	$\begin{array}{r} 24 \\ -17 \\ \hline \end{array}$	$\begin{array}{r} 60 \\ -20 \\ \hline \end{array}$	$\begin{array}{r} 86 \\ -27 \\ \hline \end{array}$	$\begin{array}{r} 93 \\ -26 \\ \hline \end{array}$	$\begin{array}{r} 52 \\ -17 \\ \hline \end{array}$	$\begin{array}{r} 47 \\ -28 \\ \hline \end{array}$
5.	$\begin{array}{r} 86 \\ -38 \\ \hline \end{array}$	$\begin{array}{r} 45 \\ -18 \\ \hline \end{array}$	$\begin{array}{r} 42 \\ -19 \\ \hline \end{array}$	$\begin{array}{r} 96 \\ -39 \\ \hline \end{array}$	$\begin{array}{r} 63 \\ -27 \\ \hline \end{array}$	$\begin{array}{r} 87 \\ -68 \\ \hline \end{array}$
6.	$\begin{array}{r} 53 \\ -17 \\ \hline \end{array}$	$\begin{array}{r} 92 \\ -45 \\ \hline \end{array}$	$\begin{array}{r} 86 \\ -18 \\ \hline \end{array}$	$\begin{array}{r} 72 \\ -17 \\ \hline \end{array}$	$\begin{array}{r} 63 \\ -45 \\ \hline \end{array}$	$\begin{array}{r} 52 \\ -13 \\ \hline \end{array}$

Lesson 1.7 Adding Three Numbers

Add the ones.   Add the tens.

```
  2 3        3  ⟍                    1             1
  4 7        7   ⟍    1 0          2 3          2 3    addend
+ 1 6      + 6        + 6          4 7          4 7    addend
           ____    _____         + 1 6        + 1 6  addend
                   1 6  or 10 + 6    _____       _____
                                       6          8 6  sum
```

___

Add.

	a	**b**	**c**	**d**	**e**	**f**
1.	1 3 2 6 +4 5 <u>8 4</u>	7 2 9 +5 6	1 6 2 3 +2 5	2 7 7 +3 4	6 1 3 +2 9	1 0 3 0 +5 0
2.	2 2 3 1 +4 5	1 9 2 1 +3 2	2 9 1 6 +1 5	1 3 1 5 +2 5	4 2 2 1 + 8	2 6 2 3 +3 5
3.	1 1 3 0 +4 2	2 7 1 6 + 9	4 7 +8	3 4 1 6 +4 1	1 6 2 3 +3 5	2 9 3 1 +2 5
4.	8 2 5 + 9	3 3 4 7 +1 2	8 6 5 + 2	1 8 3 2 +1 6	4 6 2 9 +1 6	5 3 2 1 +1 5
5.	6 6 2 1 + 8	4 7 1 3 + 8	2 2 4 1 +2 8	2 3 1 5 +1 7	1 8 1 6 +2 4	2 3 3 5 +1 7

Lesson 1.8 Addition and Subtraction Practice

Add or subtract.

	a	b	c	d	e	f
1.	23 −10	76 +21	82 −19	16 7 +13	16 +35	76 −30
2.	20 +50	30 −13	16 13 +23	76 −43	87 −45	92 −79
3.	26 +58	96 −17	72 + 3	79 + 8	16 − 8	18 12 +42
4.	86 −19	77 +16	43 −29	16 + 7	82 −42	86 −39
5.	57 −43	9 +9	0 +30	41 −22	18 42 +13	18 +53
6.	81 −79	27 +34	86 +13	92 −36	37 −24	86 + 5

Lesson 1.9 Problem Solving

Solve each problem.

1. Philip has 52 marbles. His friend, Edgar, has 39 marbles. How many marbles do they have in all?

   Philip has _____ marbles.

   Edgar has _____ marbles.

   They have _____ marbles in all.

2. Susan has 3 cats. George has 23 fish. Maria has 2 birds. How many pets do they have together?

   Susan has _____ cats.

   George has _____ fish.

   Maria has _____ birds.

   Together they have _____ pets.

3. Mr. Williams' third-grade class has 27 students. Mrs. Nakagawa's third-grade class has 31 students. How many third-grade students are there?

   Mr. Williams has _____ students.

   Mrs. Nakagawa has _____ students.

   Together, there are _____ students.

4. There are 36 adults and 17 children at the movie theater. How many people are at the movie theater?

   There are _____ people at the movie theater.

5. Kyle has 77 baseball trading cards. If Omar gives Kyle 13 baseball trading cards, how many trading cards will Kyle have?

   Kyle will have _____ baseball trading cards.

1.

2.

3.

4.

5.

Lesson 1.10 Problem Solving

SHOW YOUR WORK

Solve each problem.

1. Mrs. Lopez has 32 rose bushes in her garden. If 14 are not blooming, how many are blooming?

   Mrs. Lopez has _____ rose bushes in her garden.

   There are _____ bushes that are not blooming.

   There are _____ bushes that are blooming.

2. Tamika has 15 cousins. If 11 of her cousins are girls, how many of her cousins are boys?

   Tamika has _____ cousins.

   She has _____ cousins who are girls.

   Tamika has _____ cousins who are boys.

3. There are 76 seats on the plane. There are 62 passengers on the plane. How many empty seats are on the plane?

   There are _____ seats on the plane.

   There are _____ passengers.

   There are _____ empty seats on the plane.

4. There are 56 books on the bookshelf. If 39 are not mystery books, how many are mystery books?

   There are _____ mystery books on the bookshelf.

5. My book has 38 pages in it. If there are 12 pages that have pictures, how many pages do not have pictures?

   There are _____ pages in the book that do not have pictures.

1.

2.

3.

4.   5.

Check What You Learned

Adding and Subtracting 1- and 2-Digit Numbers (with renaming)

Add.

	a	b	c	d	e	f
1.	23 +47	17 +22	18 +53	6 +27	30 +50	27 + 0
2.	86 +12	63 +29	13 +37	47 +23	19 +29	63 +21
3.	25 +35	5 +31	20 + 0	49 +26	33 +44	46 +53
4.	86 + 5	75 + 6	13 12 +23	63 19 + 8	11 22 +33	16 32 +11

Subtract.

	a	b	c	d	e	f
5.	93 − 5	76 −13	82 −45	67 −41	14 −12	63 − 0
6.	87 −19	28 −13	65 −42	57 −35	63 −14	39 −25
7.	46 −23	80 −20	65 − 9	92 −45	99 −35	86 −19
8.	53 −45	39 −23	86 −14	92 −47	85 −45	62 −37

Check What You Learned

SHOW YOUR WORK

Adding and Subtracting 1- and 2-Digit Numbers (with renaming)

Solve each problem.

9. At an air show there were 32 airplanes in the sky. If 15 airplanes landed, how many were still in the sky?

There were _____ airplanes still in the sky.

9.

10. One bag of rocks weighs 15 pounds. Another bag of rocks weighs 23 pounds. How much do both bags of rocks weigh?

Together, the bags of rocks weigh _____ pounds.

10.

11. There were 46 people at the train station. Then, 27 people got on the train. How many people are still at the train station?

There are _____ people still at the train station.

11.

12. Sally has 32 cupcakes. She gave cupcakes to 16 people. How many cupcakes does she have left?

Sally has _____ cupcakes left.

12.

13. The car dealer had 17 model cars. Yesterday, he sold 9 of the model cars. How many model cars does he have left?

The car dealer has _____ model cars left.

13.

14. Beatrix had invited 26 people to her party. Only 9 people could not come to the party. How many people will be at Beatrix's party?

There will be _____ people at Beatrix's party.

14.

NAME _____

Check What You Know

Adding and Subtracting 2- and 3-Digit Numbers (with renaming)

Add.

	a	b	c	d	e	f
1.	27 +43	86 +92	135 + 47	82 +13	45 +154	87 +196
2.	387 +405	786 +193	150 +270	863 + 42	323 + 46	76 +84
3.	32 +196	46 +231	87 +121	76 +93	23 +54	186 +231
4.	65 +15	28 +93	57 +761	192 +775	423 +176	23 +45

Subtract.

	a	b	c	d	e	f
5.	123 − 15	87 −23	545 − 35	79 −63	187 − 93	782 −143
6.	898 −454	763 −321	981 −133	725 −123	805 − 73	120 − 80
7.	76 −41	87 −35	72 −35	153 − 92	763 −154	876 −450
8.	879 − 69	87 −43	100 − 35	730 −300	765 −231	845 −708

Grade 3

Check What You Know
Chapter 2
19

Check What You Know

SHOW YOUR WORK

Adding and Subtracting 2- and 3-Digit Numbers (with renaming)

Solve each problem.

9. Kurt has saved 29 dollars to buy a remote control car. The remote control car that he wants to buy costs 43 dollars. How much more money does he need to save?

Are you to add or subtract? _____

He will need to save _____ more dollars.

10. Latisha sold 36 candy bars on Friday and 45 candy bars on Saturday. How many candy bars did she sell in all?

Are you to add or subtract? _____

Latisha sold _____ candy bars in all.

11. Harry had 57 pennies and 16 dimes. How many coins does he have?

Are you to add or subtract? _____

He has _____ coins.

12. Tawna has 253 pennies. Shawn has 146 pennies. How many more pennies does Tawna have than Shawn?

Tawna has _____ more pennies than Shawn.

13. The team sold 453 tickets for the game. There were 249 adult tickets sold. How many children's tickets were sold?

The team sold _____ children's tickets.

9.

10.

11.

12.

13.

Lesson 2.1 Adding 2-Digit Numbers

	Add the ones.		Add the tens.

$$
\begin{array}{r} 75 \\ +66 \\ \hline \end{array}
\qquad
\begin{array}{r} {}^{1} \\ 75 \\ +66 \\ \hline \end{array}
\qquad
\begin{array}{r} {}^{1} \\ 75 \\ +\ 66 \\ \hline 141 \end{array}
\ \begin{array}{l} \text{addend} \\ \text{addend} \\[4pt] \text{sum} \end{array}
$$

$$5 + 6 = 11$$

Add.

	a	**b**	**c**	**d**	**e**	**f**
1.	23 +95 118	17 +86	90 +50	72 +46	87 +23	97 +65
2.	19 +75	26 +93	47 +58	54 +59	64 +94	87 +27
3.	23 +79	38 +81	75 +86	23 +92	86 +41	39 +82
4.	43 +71	65 +39	37 +82	19 +83	43 +62	75 +95
5.	60 +40	20 +87	23 +97	26 +85	94 +45	23 +63
6.	67 +72	95 +92	83 +67	49 +69	27 +99	82 +57

Lesson 2.1 Problem Solving

SHOW YOUR WORK

Solve each problem.

1. Sarah earned 58 dollars last week from her paper route. This week she earned 47 dollars. How much money did she earn for both weeks combined?

   She earned _____ dollars last week.

   She earned _____ dollars this week.

   She earned _____ dollars for both weeks combined.

2. Eduardo has 72 dollars in his savings account. How much money will be in his savings account if he deposits 43 dollars today?

   He has _____ dollars.

   He will deposit _____ dollars.

   He will have a total of _____ dollars in his savings account.

3. Flo read a book with 92 pages. Sofia read a book with 87 pages. How many pages did they both read?

   Flo read _____ pages.

   Sofia read _____ pages.

   Together they read _____ pages.

4. At the wedding reception there were 77 adults and 52 children. How many people were at the wedding reception?

   There were _____ adults.

   There were _____ children.

   There were _____ people at the wedding reception.

1.

2.

3.

4.

NAME _____

Lesson 2.2 Subtracting 2 Digits from 3 Digits

	Subtract the ones.	To subtract the tens, rename the 1 hundred and 2 tens as "12 tens."	Subtract the tens.	
1 2 5 − 8 4	1 2 5 − 8 4 1	0 12 X̸ 2̸ 5 − 8 4 1	0 12 X̸ 2̸ 5 − 8 4 4 1	minuend subtrahend difference

Subtract.

	a	b	c	d	e	f
1.	1 7 3 − 3 3 1 4 0	1 2 1 − 6 0	1 9 5 − 4 4	1 2 2 − 1 1	1 4 7 − 5 3	1 8 2 − 9 0
2.	1 4 3 − 6 2	1 8 0 − 7 0	1 1 9 − 1 5	1 2 3 − 1 2	1 8 6 − 6 5	1 8 7 − 4 2
3.	1 5 4 − 1 3	1 2 7 − 8 3	1 8 7 − 6 7	1 3 5 − 4 2	1 1 5 − 2 4	1 7 1 − 6 0
4.	1 3 2 − 5 1	1 7 7 − 4 3	1 9 2 − 7 1	1 8 6 − 9 2	1 3 4 − 7 2	1 2 5 − 4 5
5.	1 2 9 − 8 6	1 7 6 − 7 5	1 2 0 − 4 0	1 9 4 − 5 3	1 8 9 − 6 2	1 3 4 − 4 2
6.	1 6 5 − 5 1	1 6 7 − 4 5	1 5 0 − 3 0	1 5 7 − 6 3	1 4 9 − 6 1	1 3 9 − 6 2
7.	1 7 5 − 8 2	1 6 7 − 4 3	1 3 3 − 4 1	1 4 8 − 7 8	1 6 5 − 4 3	1 2 8 − 5 7

Lesson 2.2 Subtracting 2 Digits from 3 Digits

Rename 5 tens and 3 ones as "4 tens and 13 ones."	Subtract the ones.	Rename 1 hundred and 4 tens as "14 tens."	Subtract the tens.

$$\begin{array}{r} 1\,5\,3 \\ -\ \ 6\,5 \\ \hline \end{array}$$

$$\begin{array}{r} {}^{4\ 13}\\ 1\,\cancel{5}\,\cancel{3} \\ -\ \ 6\,5 \\ \hline \end{array}$$

$$\begin{array}{r} {}^{4\ 13}\\ 1\,\cancel{5}\,\cancel{3} \\ -\ \ 6\,5 \\ \hline 8 \end{array}$$

$$\begin{array}{r} {}^{0\ 14\,13}\\ \cancel{1}\,\cancel{5}\,\cancel{3} \\ -\ \ 6\,5 \\ \hline 8 \end{array}$$

$$\begin{array}{r} {}^{0\ 14\,13}\\ \cancel{1}\,\cancel{5}\,\cancel{3} \quad\text{minuend}\\ -\ \ 6\,5 \quad\text{subtrahend}\\ \hline 8\,8 \quad\text{difference} \end{array}$$

Subtract.

	a	b	c	d	e	f
1.	162 − 73 = 89	175 − 97	182 − 94	103 − 17	116 − 39	127 − 88
2.	174 − 95	147 − 68	132 − 65	115 − 49	107 − 39	181 − 95
3.	101 − 75	100 − 92	127 − 79	133 − 44	142 − 73	135 − 47
4.	141 − 63	137 − 79	142 − 73	153 − 67	155 − 96	164 − 88
5.	100 − 72	106 − 48	117 − 88	124 − 66	163 − 89	180 − 93
6.	172 − 87	161 − 92	145 − 66	132 − 57	130 − 43	120 − 62
7.	164 − 85	152 − 63	144 − 87	157 − 69	123 − 45	174 − 87

Lesson 2.3 Adding 3-Digit Numbers

	Add the ones.	Add the tens.	Add the hundreds.
755 +469	¹ 755 +469 4	¹ ¹ 755 +469 24	¹ ¹ 755 + 469 1224

Add.

	a	b	c	d	e	f
1.	123 562 685	982 +171	342 +591	782 +341	123 +321	681 +975
2.	862 -313	900 +130	720 +850	931 +111	823 +457	547 +321
3.	861 +421	862 +139	431 +250	782 +191	751 +605	871 +323
4.	791 +191	144 +800	192 +175	257 +147	203 +211	541 +693
5	705 +719	641 +209	873 +505	700 +650	105 +341	450 +362
.	593 +741	861 +209	735 +145	820 +431	738 +387	719 +120
7.	153 +312	712 +210	619 +715	205 +316	153 +814	613 +261

Lesson 2.3 Problem Solving

Solve each problem.

1. At the basketball game, 232 adult tickets were sold and 179 children's tickets were sold. How many tickets were sold for the basketball game?

   There were _____ adult tickets sold.

   There were _____ children's tickets sold.

   There were _____ total tickets sold.

2. At the local elementary school there are 543 boys and 476 girls. How many total students are there?

   There are _____ boys.

   There are _____ girls.

   There are _____ total students.

3. Mr. Gomez has 639 blue tiles and 722 green tiles. How many blue and green tiles does Mr. Gomez have?

   Mr. Gomez has _____ blue tiles.

   He has _____ green tiles.

   He has _____ blue and green tiles.

4. The shoe store has 324 pairs of athletic shoes and 187 pairs of sandals. How many athletic shoes and sandals does the shoe store have in all?

   There are _____ pairs of athletic shoes.

   There are _____ pairs of sandals.

   There are _____ pairs of athletic shoes and sandals in all.

1.

2.

3.

4.

Lesson 2.4 Subtracting 3-Digit Numbers

Rename 2 tens and 1 one as "1 ten and 11 ones." Then, subtract the ones.	Rename 6 hundreds and 1 ten as "5 hundreds and 11 tens." Then, subtract the tens.	Subtract the hundreds.

$$
\begin{array}{r} 621 \\ -259 \\ \hline \end{array}
\qquad
\begin{array}{r} {}^{1\,11}6\,\cancel{2}\,\cancel{1} \\ -2\,5\,9 \\ \hline 2 \end{array}
\qquad
\begin{array}{r} {}^{11}{}_{5}\,\cancel{6}\,\cancel{2}\,\cancel{1} \\ -2\,5\,9 \\ \hline 6\,2 \end{array}
\qquad
\begin{array}{r} {}^{11}{}_{5}\,\cancel{6}\,\cancel{2}\,\cancel{1} \\ -2\,5\,9 \\ \hline 3\,6\,2 \end{array}
\begin{array}{l} \text{minuend} \\ \text{subtrahend} \\ \text{difference} \end{array}
$$

Subtract.

	a	b	c	d	e	f
1.	321 −109 212	745 −152	639 −150	830 −710	626 −146	457 −309
2.	729 −321	657 −451	386 −107	411 −305	486 −109	311 −121
3.	983 −652	971 −572	876 −357	549 −360	721 −144	958 −637
4.	256 −142	347 −139	725 −196	863 −692	980 −532	720 −500
5.	543 −457	762 −135	132 −107	921 −571	631 −545	982 −144
6.	531 −250	720 −371	582 −357	793 −457	612 −483	592 −107

Lesson 2.4 Problem Solving

Solve each problem.

1. There are 990 seats at the stadium. If there are 587 people at the stadium, how many empty seats are there?

There are _____ stadium seats.

There are _____ people.

There are _____ empty seats.

2. A bicycle cost 530 dollars. There is a rebate for 147 dollars. How much will the bike cost after the rebate?

The bicycle costs _____ dollars.

The rebate is _____ dollars.

The cost of the bicycle after the rebate is

_____ dollars.

3. There were 600 green and yellow paper clips in the package. If 230 were green, how many were yellow?

There were a total of _____ paper clips.

There were _____ green paper clips.

There were _____ yellow paper clips.

4. The ice-cream store sold 349 scoops of ice-cream on Monday. The store sold 178 scoops of ice-cream on Tuesday. How many more scoops did the store sell on Monday?

The ice-cream store sold _____ more scoops on Monday than on Tuesday.

5. Last year, Randy received a set of 360 toy cars. This year, Randy counted only 163 toy cars in his set. How many toy cars had Randy lost?

Randy lost _____ toy cars.

1.

2.

3.

4.

5.

Lesson 2.5 Thinking Subtraction for Addition

To check

215 + 109 = 324,

subtract 109 from 324.

```
  2 1 5  ◄-----┐
+ 1 0 9        ┊
-------        ┊   These should be the same.
  3 2 4        ┊
- 1 0 9        ┊
-------        ┊
  2 1 5  ◄-----┘
```

Add. Check each answer.

	a	b	c	d	e	f
1.	1 5 7 + 2 1 2 --- 3 6 9 - 2 1 2 --- 1 5 7	7 1 9 + 1 8 2	3 1 2 + 1 0 5	2 1 3 + 5 1 9	3 0 6 + 2 1 5	1 2 0 + 1 7 0
2.	7 1 0 + 3 9 8	3 5 7 + 2 4 9	7 1 2 + 3 6 3	7 1 4 + 2 9 1	3 1 2 + 8 5	4 1 9 + 5 7
3.	3 0 0 + 5 4 7	5 9 1 + 1 2 0	6 1 2 + 3 1 9	4 2 5 + 1 2 5	4 1 1 + 1 2 0	2 4 7 + 2 5 9
4.	8 6 3 + 1 9 2	4 5 9 + 1 3 0	6 0 3 + 2 0 9	7 1 1 + 1 9 1	2 5 2 + 1 3 0	4 1 2 + 2 8 3

Lesson 2.6 Thinking Addition for Subtraction

To check

982 − 657 = 325,

add 657 to 325.

```
  982  ◄---┐
 −657      ¦
 ─────     ¦
  325      ¦   These should be the same.
 +657      ¦
 ─────     ¦
  982  ◄---┘
```

Subtract. Check each answer.

	a	**b**	**c**	**d**	**e**	**f**
1.	720 −150 ─── 570 +150 ─── 720	321 − 83	125 − 92	983 −657	456 −291	442 −220
2.	300 −179	119 −104	423 −197	259 −147	592 −463	708 −412
3.	519 −120	540 −320	192 − 86	710 −447	683 −419	712 −307
4.	719 −532	919 −457	687 −250	912 −609	542 −327	728 −530

Check What You Learned

Adding and Subtracting 2- and 3-Digit Numbers (with renaming)

Add.

	a	b	c	d	e	f
1.	75 +92	135 +210	193 + 56	310 + 92	513 +409	746 +122
2.	193 + 86	183 +192	842 +908	109 +236	963 +310	15? +21?
3.	512 +457	310 + 97	510 +346	910 +132	512 +403	9?2 + ?8
4.	543 +286	123 +592	647 +382	442 + 85	123 210 +392	12? 91? +407

CHAPTER 2 POSTTEST

Subtract.

	a	b	c	d	e	f
5.	172 − 35	192 − 86	174 − 96	120 − 80	310 − 40	293 −107
6.	986 −698	862 −245	352 −121	187 − 72	647 −253	547 −183
7.	662 −503	708 −231	456 −269	882 −199	753 −268	712 −543
8.	712 −402	548 −213	593 −369	610 −132	782 −441	192 − 85

Check What You Learned

Adding and Subtracting 2- and 3-Digit Numbers (with renaming)

CHAPTER 2 POSTTEST

Solve each problem.

9. For a game of checkers, 24 checkers are needed. There are only 18 checkers in the box. How many checkers are missing?

There are _____ checkers missing.

9.

10. An adult has 32 teeth. A child has 24 teeth. How many more teeth does an adult have?

An adult has _____ more teeth than a child.

10.

11. Sam weighed 232 pounds. He lost 13 pounds. How much does Sam weigh now?

Sam weighs _____ pounds.

11.

12. Alvin has 532 pennies. Regina has 691 pennies. How many pennies do they have together?

Alvin and Regina have _____ pennies together.

12.

13. Mr. Ito is 53 years old. His daughter, Kimi, is 25. How much older is Mr. Ito than his daughter?

Mr. Ito is _____ years older than his daughter.

13.

14. Mr. and Mrs. Acosta have been married for 47 years. Mrs. Acosta was 29 when she married Mr. Acosta. How old is Mrs. Acosta now?

Mrs. Acosta is _____ years old.

14.

Check What You Know

Adding and Subtracting to 4-Digit Numbers (with renaming)

Add or subtract.

	a	b	c	d	e
1.	13 7 +19	23 42 +97	22 24 +16	8 9 +5	21 47 +58
2.	123 415 +423	190 180 +360	420 567 +321	519 612 +313	423 521 +747
3.	1436 +5120	5190 +4125	5032 +1764	4321 +2841	5960 +4011
4.	1340 − 380	1960 − 420	720 −340	5120 −1780	4963 −1082
5.	5947 −4272	5803 −1992	1906 −1173	1876 − 759	4120 −3290
6.	9645 −6823	312 − 20	421 − 30	1500 −1200	4500 − 720

Round each number to the place named.

	a	b	c	d
7.	543 tens	867 hundreds	479 tens	962 hundreds
	_____	_____	_____	_____

NAME _____

Check What You Know

Adding and Subtracting to 4-Digit Numbers (with renaming)

Solve each problem.

8. Gerod has 5 birds, 3 turtles, 2 hamsters, and 1 dog. How many pets does he have?

   Gerod has _____ pets.

8.

9. Oleta has 19 dimes, 27 quarters, 153 pennies, and 6 nickels. How many coins does she have?

   Oleta has _____ coins.

9.

10. In the year 1998, an antique vase was 239 years old. In what year was the vase made?

    The vase was made in the year _____.

10.

11. During his walk each day, Paul counted his steps. In 4 days, he walked 420, 980, 642, and 760 steps. How many steps did he walk?

    Paul walked _____ steps in 4 days.

11.

12. James received 100 dollars for his birthday. He spent 63 dollars of it on two computer games. Estimate how much money he has left.

    James has about _____ dollars left.

12.

13. At a basketball game, one team scored 36 points. The other team scored 27 points. Estimate the total points scored in the game.

    There were a total of about _____ points scored in the basketball game.

13.

Lesson 3.3 Adding 4-Digit Numbers

	Add the ones.	Add the tens.	Add the hundreds.	Add the thousands.
3746 +5899	¹ 3746 +5899 5	¹ ¹ 3746 +5899 45	¹ ¹ ¹ 3746 +5899 645	¹ ¹ ¹ 3746 +5899 9645

Add.

	a	b	c	d	e	f
1.	7865 +1192 9057	8654 +1219	4320 +3069	3543 +3921	4293 +5176	6405 +3398
2.	1982 +1782	7083 +2907	4325 +4986	6057 +1239	8761 +1032	2305 +5747
3.	3050 +4707	6932 +2349	5437 +2968	1718 +2347	7923 +1250	4523 +3962
4.	5431 +2989	7986 +1479	1119 +2459	7239 +1635	2450 +7267	6527 +2985
5.	5431 +1982	7986 +1246	1543 +3989	7121 +1923	8763 +1005	4321 +2387
6.	5450 +1987	4733 +2576	3981 +2877	6986 +2928	7181 +2111	7900 +2005

Lesson 3.3 Problem Solving

Solve each problem.

1. Two local high schools have 1,523 students and 1,695 students. How many students are there at both high schools together?

One high school has _____ students.

The other high school has _____ students.

There are a total of _____ students at both high schools.

2. Monica started at an elevation of 1,200 feet for her hiking trip. She hiked up the mountain for 1,320 feet in elevation. How high did she hike?

Monica started at _____ feet in elevation.

She hiked _____ feet in elevation.

She hiked up to an elevation of _____ feet.

3. Steve has a coin worth 1,050 dollars. He has another coin worth 1,072 dollars. How much are both coins worth?

Both coins are worth _____ dollars.

4. Roy ran 1,100 yards as a running back during his junior year of high school. During his senior year of high school, he ran 1,500 yards as a running back. How many yards did he run in both years combined?

Roy ran a total of _____ yards for both his junior and senior year of high school.

1.

2.

3.

4.

Lesson 3.4 Subtracting to 4 Digits

| Subtract the ones. | Rename 4 hundreds and 3 tens as "3 hundreds and 13 tens." Subtract the tens. | Rename 5 thousands and 3 hundreds as "4 thousands and 13 hundreds." Subtract the hundreds. | Subtract the thousands. |

$$
\begin{array}{r} 5437 \\ -1592 \\ \hline \end{array}
\quad
\begin{array}{r} 5437 \\ -1592 \\ \hline 5 \end{array}
\quad
\begin{array}{r} 5\overset{3}{\cancel{4}}\overset{13}{\cancel{3}}7 \\ -1592 \\ \hline 45 \end{array}
\quad
\begin{array}{r} \overset{4}{\cancel{5}}\overset{\overset{13}{3}}{\cancel{4}}\overset{13}{\cancel{3}}7 \\ -1592 \\ \hline 845 \end{array}
\quad
\begin{array}{r} \overset{4}{\cancel{5}}\overset{\overset{13}{3}}{\cancel{4}}\overset{13}{\cancel{3}}7 \\ -1592 \\ \hline 3845 \end{array}
$$

Subtract.

	a	b	c	d	e
1.	9865 −2382 **7483**	7528 − 792	8654 −3993	1925 − 183	1876 − 982
2.	5473 −3591	8762 − 682	7945 − 963	8654 − 772	7846 −3974
3.	6932 −2840	1389 − 794	2545 − 963	7863 −2572	8121 − 640
4.	7865 − 974	3456 − 661	7982 − 490	8163 −4670	4325 −1534
5.	9876 − 985	8716 −5823	5432 −3651	3287 − 395	7805 − 164
6.	5439 − 767	4321 − 841	7865 − 974	7976 −4682	5439 − 866

Lesson 3.4 Problem Solving

Solve each problem.

1. There are 2,532 students at the school. 1,341 are girls. How many are boys?

There are _____ students.

There are _____ girls.

There are _____ boys.

2. In 2013, the average rent for a house was 1,250 dollars per month. In 1944, the average rent for a house was 495 dollars per month. How much higher was the rent in 2013 than in 1944?

Rent in 2013 was _____ dollars per month.

Rent in 1944 was _____ dollars per month.

Rent in 2013 was _____ dollars per month higher than in 1944.

3. In the year 1986, Mrs. Olveras turned 103 years old. In what year was she born?

In the year _____,

Mrs. Olveras turned _____ years old.

Mrs. Olveras was born in _____.

4. In the year 1996, Mr. Smith's car was considered a classic. The car was made in 1942. How old is Mr. Smith's car?

Mr. Smith's car is _____ years old.

5. Kayla wants to visit her grandmother who lives 2,583 miles away. The airplane will only take her 2,392 miles toward her destination. Kayla needs to rent a car to drive the remaining miles. How many miles does Kayla need to drive?

Kayla would need to drive _____ miles.

1.

2.

3.

4.   **5.**

Lesson 3.6 Estimating Addition

Round each number to the highest place value the numbers have in common. Then, add from right to left.

$$194 \longrightarrow 190$$
$$+\ \ 76 \longrightarrow +\ \ 80$$
$$\overline{\hphantom{+00}270}$$

$$203 \longrightarrow 200$$
$$+196 \longrightarrow +200$$
$$\overline{\hphantom{+00}400}$$

The highest place value for 194 and 76 is the tens place. Round 194 and 76 to the tens place. Add.

The highest place value for 203 and 196 is the hundreds place. Round 203 and 196 to the hundreds place. Add.

Estimate each sum to the nearest ten.

	a		b	c	d
1.	25	30	23	57	42
	+36	+40	+14	+51	+92
		70			

2.	92		131	165	147
	+51		+ 42	+ 92	+ 97

Estimate each sum to the nearest hundred.

3.	147	100	175	457	543
	+362	+400	+302	+603	+261
		500			

4.	1132		1250	5786	4679
	+ 432		+ 347	+ 432	+ 578

Estimate each sum to the nearest thousand.

5.	1562	2000	6054	3541	2795
	+3492	+3000	+6542	+7987	+2454
		5000			

Lesson 3.6 Problem Solving

Solve each problem by using estimation.

1. Kirima read 534 pages last week and 352 pages this week. About how many pages did Kirima read?

Kirima read about _____ pages.

2. Tim has 13 dollars. James has 15 dollars. About how many dollars do they have together?

Tim and James have about _____ dollars together.

3. Mr. Hwan had 532 dollars in his savings account before he made a deposit of 259 dollars. About how much money does he have in his savings account now?

Mr. Hwan has about _____ dollars in his savings account now.

4. Mrs. Luna is 43 years old. Mrs. Turner is 52 years old. Mrs. Rockwell is 39 years old. About how much is their combined age?

Their combined age is about _____ years.

5. Marla bought 4 boards at the home center. The boards were 86, 103, 152, and 161 inches long. About how many inches of boards did Marla buy? Round to the nearest ten.

Marla bought about _____ inches of boards.

1.	
2.	
3.	
4.	
5.	

Lesson 3.7 Estimating Subtraction

Round each number to the highest place value the numbers have in common. Then, subtract from right to left.

$$
\begin{array}{r}
236 \longrightarrow 240 \\
-\ 49 \longrightarrow -\ 50 \\
\hline
190
\end{array}
\qquad
\begin{array}{r}
396 \longrightarrow 400 \\
-287 \longrightarrow -300 \\
\hline
100
\end{array}
$$

The highest place value for 236 and 49 is the tens place. Round 236 and 49 to the tens place. Subtract.

The highest place value for 396 and 287 is the hundreds place. Round 396 and 287 to the hundreds place. Subtract.

Estimate each difference to the nearest ten.

	a	b	c	d
1.	$\begin{array}{r}56 \quad 60 \\ -43 \quad -40 \\ \hline 20\end{array}$	$\begin{array}{r}49 \\ -12 \\ \hline\end{array}$	$\begin{array}{r}72 \\ -61 \\ \hline\end{array}$	$\begin{array}{r}80 \\ -45 \\ \hline\end{array}$
2.	$\begin{array}{r}451 \\ -\ 72 \\ \hline\end{array}$	$\begin{array}{r}986 \\ -\ 59 \\ \hline\end{array}$	$\begin{array}{r}760 \\ -\ 32 \\ \hline\end{array}$	$\begin{array}{r}542 \\ -\ 57 \\ \hline\end{array}$

Estimate each difference to the nearest hundred.

	a	b	c	d
3.	$\begin{array}{r}543 \quad 500 \\ -290 \quad -300 \\ \hline 200\end{array}$	$\begin{array}{r}943 \\ -457 \\ \hline\end{array}$	$\begin{array}{r}547 \\ -249 \\ \hline\end{array}$	$\begin{array}{r}686 \\ -162 \\ \hline\end{array}$
4.	$\begin{array}{r}1543 \\ -\ 661 \\ \hline\end{array}$	$\begin{array}{r}3247 \\ -\ 843 \\ \hline\end{array}$	$\begin{array}{r}4560 \\ -\ 493 \\ \hline\end{array}$	$\begin{array}{r}7631 \\ -\ 647 \\ \hline\end{array}$

Estimate each difference to the nearest thousand.

	a	b	c	d
5.	$\begin{array}{r}8798 \quad 9000 \\ -4453 \quad -4000 \\ \hline 5000\end{array}$	$\begin{array}{r}9476 \\ -2652 \\ \hline\end{array}$	$\begin{array}{r}7345 \\ -6443 \\ \hline\end{array}$	$\begin{array}{r}9432 \\ -1486 \\ \hline\end{array}$

Lesson 3.7 Problem Solving

SHOW YOUR WORK

Solve each problem by using estimation.

1. Fred had 39 dollars. He gave 23 dollars to Kim. About how much money does Fred have left?

Fred has about _____ dollars left.

1.

2. There are 186 apartments in an apartment building. 92 are not rented. About how many apartments are rented?

There are about _____ rented apartments.

2.

3. Sue wants to buy a bicycle for 560 dollars. She has 430 dollars. About how much more money does she need to buy the bicycle?

Sue needs about _____ more dollars to buy the bicycle.

3.

4. At the theater, 98 adult tickets were sold. If 210 tickets were sold, about how many children's tickets were sold?

About _____ children's tickets were sold.

4.

5. Kelly bought a roll of cloth 197 inches long. She cut 85 inches off the roll to use in a project. About how many inches did she have left on the roll? Round to the nearest ten.

Kelly had about _____ inches left on the roll.

5.

Solve each problem.

17. Marcella has a dog-walking business. She walked 12 dogs on Thursday, 15 dogs on Saturday, and 9 dogs on Sunday. How many dogs did Marcella walk altogether?

Marcella walked _____ dogs altogether.

18. Last week, the ice cream shop sold 188 hot fudge sundaes, 54 chocolate sundaes, and 62 strawberry sundaes. How many more hot fudge sundaes did the store sell than chocolate and strawberry combined?

The store sold _____ more hot fudge sundaes than all the others combined.

19. Owen is going to visit his aunt. He travels 278 miles on Saturday. He travels 81 miles farther on Sunday than he did on Saturday. How many miles did Owen travel on Sunday?

Owen traveled _____ miles on Sunday.

20. Delany's favorite book is *Trees in the Breeze*. The book has 85 pages of text and 145 pages of pictures. If Delany is on page 197, how many pages are left?

There are _____ pages left.

21. Joey is running a 26-mile marathon. Joey takes a break after 4 miles. He then runs 8 miles more. How many miles does Joey have left to run?

Joey has _____ miles left to run.

22. Jasper visited the zoo and saw 45 lizards, snakes, and turtles altogether. If he saw 12 lizards and 26 snakes, how many turtles did Jasper see?

Jasper saw _____ turtles.

17.	18.
19.	20.
21.	22.

Mid-Test Chapters 1–3

SHOW YOUR WORK

Solve each problem.

23. Sarah has 50 marbles and Jessie has 63 marbles. How many marbles do they have together?

Sarah and Jessie have _____ marbles together.

24. A pencil costs 48 cents and a package of gum costs 29 cents. Estimate about how much the pencil and the package of gum cost together.

The pencil and the package of gum cost about

_____ cents.

25. Gloria has saved 329 dollars. If she spends 58 dollars, how much money will she have left?

Gloria will have _____ dollars left.

26. Tito read 320 pages in a book. Akando read 323 pages in a book. Kenji read 313 pages in a book. How many pages did they read?

Tito, Akando, and Kenji read _____ pages.

27. In the year 1983, Mr. Smith was 94 years old. In what year was he born?

Mr. Smith was born in the year _____.

28. Tobias had 53 baseball cards. He gave his friends 28 of the baseball cards. Estimate how many baseball cards Tobias has left.

Tobias has about _____ baseball cards left.

29. Thirteen students from Mrs. Daley's class want to go camping. Eighteen students from Mrs. Campbell's class want to go camping. Estimate many students want to go camping altogether.

About _____ students want to go camping all together.

23.	24.
25.	26.
27.	28.
29.	

CHAPTERS 1–3 MID-TEST

Lesson 4.8 Problem Solving

Solve each problem.

1. Gary read 3 books with 60 pages each. How many pages did he read in all?

There are _____ pages in each book.

Gary read _____ books.

Gary read _____ pages in all.

1.

2. There are 4 classes at a school. Each class has 20 students. How many students are at the school?

There are _____ students in each class.

There are _____ classes.

There are _____ students in the school.

2.

3. Yolanda used up 4 rolls of stickers. If each roll has 30 stickers, how many stickers did she use in all?

Each roll has _____ stickers.

Yolanda used _____ rolls.

Yolanda used a total of _____ stickers.

3.

4. During a game, 2 teams play against each other. There are 10 players on the field for each team. How many players are on the field during the game?

There are _____ players on the field.

4.

5.

5. There are 10 apples in each basket. If Mary buys 6 baskets, how many apples does she have?

Mary has _____ apples.

Lesson 4.9 Two-Step Problem Solving **SHOW YOUR WORK**

Make a mental computation first. Then, solve the problem.

The PE teacher gave each team 6 basketballs and 6 tennis balls. If there were 5 teams, how many total balls did the PE teacher give out?

Each team gets 6 of each type of ball. I know that 6 times 5 is 30, so that is 30 basketballs and 30 tennis balls. Then, I can add the balls together, and 30 plus 30 is 60. So, there are 60 balls in all.

$$\begin{array}{r} 6 \\ \times\ 5 \\ \hline 30 \end{array} \qquad \begin{array}{r} 30 \\ +30 \\ \hline 60 \end{array}$$

Mental Computation: 60

1. Eight girls and 5 boys each have a button collection. Each girl has 8 buttons in her collection, and each boy has 4 buttons in his collection. How many buttons altogether do the boys and girls have?

   Mental Computation: _____

   The boys and girls have _____ buttons altogether.

   1.

2. There are 2 rows of 5 computers in each office. If there are 7 offices in the building, how many computers are in the building altogether?

   Mental Computation: _____

   There are _____ computers in the building.

   2.

3. Kayla bought 5 bags of dried mango slices. Each bag has 7 slices. How many mango slices does Kayla have left over after she gives away 10 slices?

   Mental Computation: _____

   Kayla has _____ mango slices left.

   3.

4. Jin bought 7 boxes of Mixed Mints and 4 boxes of Fudge Crunchies. Each Mixed Mints box has 10 cookies and each Fudge Crunchies box has 7. How many cookies does Jin have altogether?

   Mental Computation: _____

   Jin has _____ cookies altogether.

   4.

Lesson 5.1 Understanding Division

$\overline{)}$ means divide.

$$\begin{array}{r} 6 \leftarrow \text{quotient} \\ \text{divisor} \longrightarrow 3\overline{)18} \leftarrow \text{dividend} \end{array}$$

$3\overline{)18}^{\ 6}$ is read "18 divided by 3 is equal to 6."

$4\overline{)12}^{\ 3}$ is read "12 divided by 4 is equal to 3."

In $4\overline{)12}^{\ 3}$, the divisor is 4, the dividend is 12, and the quotient is 3.

$\div$ also means divide.

$$10 \div 2 = 5$$
dividend divisor quotient

$10 \div 2 = 5$ is read "10 divided by 2 is equal to 5."

$6 \div 3 = 2$ is read "6 divided by 3 is equal to 2."

In $6 \div 3 = 2$, the divisor is 3, the dividend is 6, and the quotient is 2.

Complete each sentence.

1. $6\overline{)12}^{\ 2}$ is read "__12__ divided by 6 is equal to __2__."

2. $8\overline{)24}^{\ 3}$ is read "___ divided by 8 is equal to ___."

3. $4\overline{)36}^{\ 9}$ is read "___ divided by 4 is equal to ___."

4. In $4\overline{)8}^{\ 2}$, the divisor is ___, the dividend is ___, and the quotient is ___.

5. In $7\overline{)35}^{\ 5}$, the divisor is ___, the dividend is ___, and the quotient is ___.

6. $20 \div 5 = 4$ is read "___ divided by 5 is equal to ___."

7. $27 \div 9 = 3$ is read "___ divided by 9 is equal to ___."

8. $6 \div 2 = 3$ is read "___ divided by 2 is equal to ___."

9. In $15 \div 3 = 5$, the divisor is ___, the dividend is ___, and the quotient is ___.

10. In $14 \div 2 = 7$, the divisor is ___, the dividend is ___, and the quotient is ___.

Lesson 5.1 Understanding Division

8 △ in all.
4 △ in each group.
How many groups?

8 ÷ 4 = 2

There are 2 groups.

△△△△
△△△△

8 △ in all.
2 groups of △.
How many △ in each group?

8 ÷ 2 = 4

There are 4 in each group.

Check by multiplication: There are 2 groups of 4.

2 × 4 = 8

Complete the following.

a   **b**

1. 12 ☐ in all.

3 ☐ in each group.

How many groups?

12 ÷ 3 = __4__

There are __4__ groups.

Check: __4 × 3 = 12__

☐☐☐
☐☐☐
☐☐☐
☐☐☐

12 ☐ in all.

4 groups of ☐.

How many in each group?

12 ÷ 4 = _____

There are _____ ☐ in each group.

Check: _____

2. 20 As in all.

_____ As in each group.

How many groups?

20 ÷ 4 = _____

There are _____ groups.

Check: _____

AAAA
AAAA
AAAA
AAAA
AAAA

20 As in all.

_____ groups of As.

How many in each group?

20 ÷ 5 = _____

There are _____ As in each group.

Check: _____

3. _____ Fs in all.

_____ Fs in each group.

How many groups?

12 ÷ 2 = _____

There are _____ groups.

Check: _____

FF
FF
FF
FF
FF
FF

_____ Fs in all.

_____ groups of Fs.

How many in each group?

12 ÷ 6 = _____

There are _____ Fs in each group.

Check: _____

Check What You Learned

Division

Solve each problem.

10. There are 64 pages in a book. There are 8 chapters in the book. Each chapter has the same number of pages. How many pages are in each chapter of the book?

There are _____ pages in each chapter of the book.

10.

11. Six horses can live in the stable. If 1 horse can live in each stall, how many stalls are in the stable?

There are _____ stalls in the stable.

11.

12. A golfer shot a score of 45 in a golf match. She played 9 holes. She had the same score at each of the holes. What was her score at each hole?

She shot a score of _____ at each hole.

12.

13. A package of 12 donuts was shared evenly among 3 friends. How many donuts did each friend receive?

Each friend received _____ donuts.

13.

14. A bicycle has 18 speeds. Each of its 2 gears has the same number of speeds. How many speeds does the bicycle have for each gear?

Each gear has _____ speeds.

14.   **15.**

15. Forty teenagers went on a river-rafting trip. If each raft held 8 teenagers, how many rafts did the teenagers have for their trip?

The teenagers had _____ rafts.

NAME _____

Check What You Know

Fractions

What fraction of each figure is shaded?

a	b	c

1.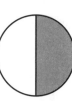

_____ _____ _____

2.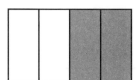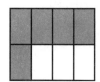

_____ _____ _____

What fraction of each set is shaded?

a	b	c

3.

_____ _____ _____

4. Label these fractions on the number line: $\frac{1}{6}$ and $\frac{4}{6}$

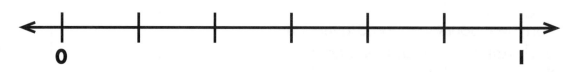

Lesson 6.2 Parts of a Set

A fraction is a number for part of a set.

$\dfrac{1}{2}$ ← numerator   (part of the set)
     ← denominator   (parts in all of the set)

   $\dfrac{1}{2}$ ← part shaded
      ← parts in all of the set

   $\dfrac{2}{3}$ ← parts shaded
      ← parts in all of the set

What fraction of each set is shaded?

	a	**b**	**c**
1.			
	$\dfrac{4}{5}$	_____	_____
2.			
	_____	_____	_____
3.			
	_____	_____	_____

Shade the number indicated by the fraction.

	a	**b**	**c**	**d**
4.				
	$\dfrac{4}{8}$	$\dfrac{3}{4}$	$\dfrac{3}{10}$	$\dfrac{1}{5}$

Lesson 6.3 Comparing Fractions

$$\frac{2}{5} > \frac{1}{5} \qquad \frac{1}{3} < \frac{1}{2} \qquad \frac{1}{4} = \frac{2}{8}$$

$\frac{2}{5}$ is greater than $\frac{1}{5}$. $\frac{1}{3}$ is less than $\frac{1}{2}$. $\frac{1}{4}$ is equal to $\frac{2}{8}$.

Use >, <, or = to compare the fractions.

	a	b	c

1.

$$\frac{1}{4} \;\bigcirc\!<\; \frac{3}{4} \qquad \frac{1}{2} \;\bigcirc\; \frac{2}{4} \qquad \frac{2}{3} \;\bigcirc\; \frac{1}{2}$$

2.

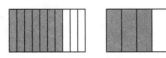

$$\frac{7}{10} \;\bigcirc\; \frac{3}{5} \qquad \frac{3}{8} \;\bigcirc\; \frac{3}{4} \qquad \frac{1}{3} \;\bigcirc\; \frac{5}{8}$$

3.

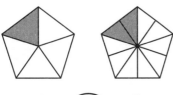

$$\frac{1}{5} \;\bigcirc\; \frac{2}{10} \qquad \frac{3}{4} \;\bigcirc\; \frac{1}{2} \qquad \frac{6}{10} \;\bigcirc\; \frac{2}{5}$$

Lesson 6.3 Comparing Fractions

What fraction of each figure is shaded? Compare the fractions. Use >, <, or =.

a	b	c

1.

$\dfrac{1}{2}$ ⟨ = ⟩ $\dfrac{2}{4}$ ◯   ◯

2.

◯   ◯   ◯

3.

     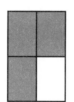   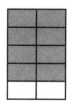

◯   ◯   ◯

Lesson 6.4 Fractions on a Number Line

Label $\frac{1}{8}$.

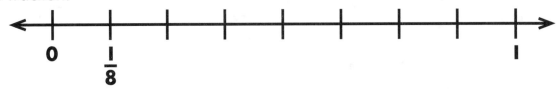

0   1

Steps
1. First, divide the number line into 8 equal parts (the denominator).
2. Next, count from zero the parts you need (the numerator).
3. Label the fraction.

0    $\frac{1}{8}$ 1

Label the fractions given.

1. $\frac{1}{4}$

0   1

2. $\frac{3}{4}$

0   1

3. $\frac{1}{3}$

0   1

4. $\frac{2}{3}$

0   1

5. $\frac{4}{4}$

0   1

Lesson 6.5 Equivalent Fractions on a Number Line

The fractions $\frac{2}{4}$ and $\frac{1}{2}$ are equivalent because they are at the same spot on the number line.

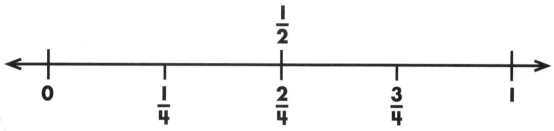

Answer the questions based on the number lines.

1. Are the fractions $\frac{1}{8}$ and $\frac{1}{4}$ equivalent? _____

   Name 2 other fractions that are equivalent. _____ _____

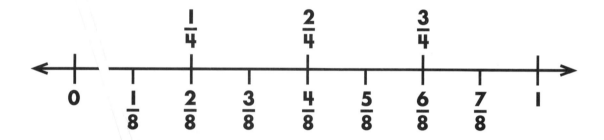

2. Are the fractions $\frac{1}{6}$ and $\frac{2}{3}$ equivalent? _____

   Name 2 other fractions that are equivalent. _____ _____

Lesson 6.6 Whole Numbers as Fractions

 $= \frac{1}{1} = 1$ 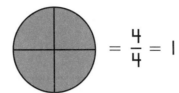 $= \frac{4}{4} = 1$ 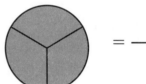 $= \frac{2}{2} = 1$

Complete the fractions and show the whole number.

1. 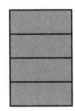 $= \frac{4}{4} = 1$

2. $= \frac{}{} =$

3.  $= \frac{}{} =$

4. $= \frac{}{} =$

5. 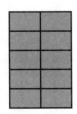 $= \frac{}{} =$

6. $= \frac{}{} =$

Check What You Learned

Fractions

What fraction of each figure is shaded?

        a   **b**   **c**

1.    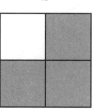   

_____   _____   _____

What fraction of each set is shaded?

        a   **b**   **c**

2.   

_____   _____   _____

Label the fractions on each number line.

3. $\dfrac{1}{4}$ and $\dfrac{3}{4}$

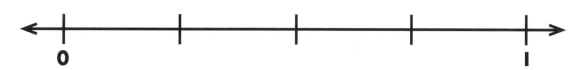

4. $\dfrac{3}{8}$ and $\dfrac{5}{8}$

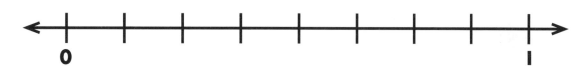

Check What You Learned

Fractions

Use >, <, or = to compare the fractions.

a	b	c

5.

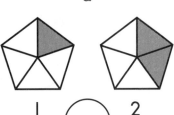  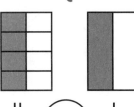

$\frac{1}{5}$ ◯ $\frac{2}{5}$ $\frac{1}{3}$ ◯ $\frac{7}{8}$ $\frac{4}{8}$ ◯ $\frac{1}{2}$

What fraction of each figure is shaded? Compare the fractions. Use >, <, or =.

a	b	c

6.

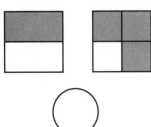 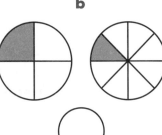 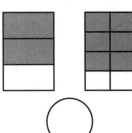

◯ ◯ ____ ____   ◯ ____ ____   ◯ ____ ____

Label the fractions on the number line.

7. $\frac{1}{3}$ and $\frac{3}{3}$

0   1

Write the fraction.

8.

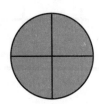 = _____ or _____

Check What You Know

Measurement

Choose an answer.

	a		b
1.	About how much water will a bucket hold?		About how much does a pencil weigh?

a. 5 inches

b. 5 pounds

c. 5 liters

a. 6 grams

b. 60 grams

c. 600 grams

Solve.

2. Kyle has 48 grams of cheese in a bag. Maria has 72 grams of cheese in a bag. How many grams of cheese do Kyle and Maria have altogether?

_____

Complete the graphs.

	a		b

3.

Favorite Sports
Baseball = 40
Soccer = 10
Football = 45

3rd Graders' Bedtimes
8:00 = 8
8:30 = 4
9:00 = 16

Favorite Sports

```
50
45
40
35
30
25
20
15
10
 5
 0
```

3rd Graders' Bedtimes	

Key _____ = 4

NAME _____

Check What You Know

Measurement

Write the area of the figure.

a

4.

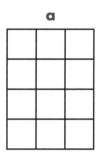

_____ sq. units

b

_____ sq. units

---

5. Draw the square units to find the area of the rectangle.

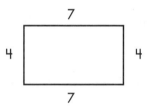

A = _____ sq. units

6. Multiply to find the area.

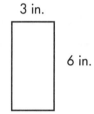

A = _____ sq. in.

---

7. Find the area.

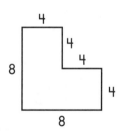

A = _____ sq. units

8. Solve.

Blake is fencing a rectangular dog pen. Two of the sides are 67 feet long, and the other two sides are 41 feet. How many feet of fencing will Blake need?

_____ ft.

Lesson 7.1 Measuring Volume and Mass

Answer each question.

1. A refrigerator weighs about: 90 grams   90 kilograms   9 kilograms

2. A wading pool holds about: 500 grams   500 liters   5,000 liters

3. A small dog weighs about: 15 grams   50 grams   5,000 grams

4. A nail weighs about: 1 gram   10 grams   100 grams

Solve.

5. Emily's bag of fruit weighs 32 ounces. Jason's bag of fruit weighs 14 ounces. How many ounces do Emily and Jason's bags weigh altogether?

   Emily and Jason's bags of fruit weigh _____ ounces altogether.

6. Vince brought 4 quarts of juice for the party. Jose brought 6 quarts of juice for the party. How many more quarts of juice did Jose bring than Vince?

   Jose brought _____ more quarts of juice than Vince.

7. Jim had 18 gallons of paint to paint his entire house. He only used 11 gallons. How many gallons of paint does Jim have left?

   Jim has _____ gallons of paint left.

8. Inez weighed 3 kilograms when she was born. Now she weighs 13 kilograms. How much weight did Inez gain since she was born?

   Inez gained _____ kilograms since she was born.

NAME _____

Lesson 7.1 Measuring Volume and Mass

Answer each question.

1. A swimming pool can hold about: 1 liter   10 liters   1,000 liters

2. A butterfly weighs about: 100 grams   1 gram   10 grams

3. A juice bottle can hold about: 2 liters   200 liters   2,000 liters

4. A chicken can weigh: 7 grams   70 grams   700 grams

Solve.

5. A carton contains 2 liters of juice. If there are 18 cartons of juice, how many liters of juice are there?

   There are _____ liters of juice.

6. A saltshaker holds 5 grams of salt. If there are 20 saltshakers in the restaurant, how many grams of salt are in the restaurant?

   There are _____ grams of salt in the restaurant.

7. Clarissa has 6 plants in her house. Each plant weighs 4 kilograms. How many kilograms do the plants weigh altogether?

   Clarissa's plants weigh _____ kilograms altogether.

8. Danny caught a fish that was 15 pounds. Ashley caught a fish that was 20 pounds. How many more pounds does Ashley's fish weigh than Danny's fish?

   Ashley's fish weighs _____ pounds more than Danny's fish.

Lesson 7.2 Drawing Picture Graphs

A **picture graph** uses symbols to represent data.

The key tells you the value of each symbol on the picture graph.

Use the frequency table to complete the graph.

Students' Hair Color

Brown	☺ ☺ ☺ ☺ ☺ ☺ ☺
Black	☺ ☺ ☺ ☺ ☺
Blonde	☺ ☺ ☺ ☺ ☺ ⸮
Red	☺ ⸮

Key: ☺ = 2 students

Frequency Table

Brown	ℍℍ ℍℍ IIII
Black	ℍℍ ℍℍ
Blonde	ℍℍ ℍℍ I
Red	III

How many students have red hair?

Each stick figure represents two students.

Count by twos when counting the stick figures in the row labeled "red." Add 1 to the sum for the half stick figure.

_____3_____ students have red hair.

Complete the picture graph. Answer the question.

Flowers In My Garden

Key: ✿ = 2 flowers

Frequency Table

Daisies	ℍℍ III
Roses	ℍℍ
Sunflowers	II

How many total flowers are in the garden? _____

Lesson 7.3 Drawing Bar Graphs

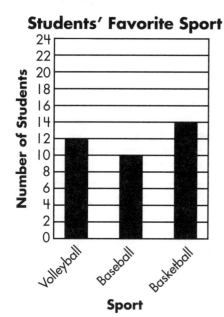

A **bar graph** uses rectangular bars to represent data.

Use the frequency table to complete the graph.

How many students chose baseball as their favorite sport?

Find the bar labeled baseball.

Follow the top of the bar to the scale at the left.

This value represents the number of students whose favorite sport is baseball.

Frequency Table

Volleyball	12
Baseball	10
Basketball	14

___10___ students chose baseball as their favorite sport.

Complete the bar graph. Answer the question.

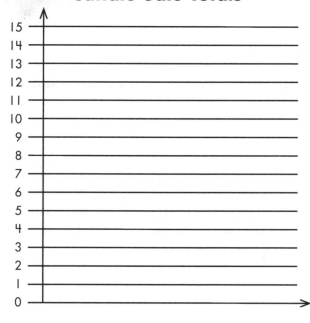

Frequency Table

Abbie	10
Brady	15
Denise	6

How many more candles did Brady

sell than Denise? _____

Lesson 7.4 Gathering Data to Draw a Line Plot

Use a ruler to measure the length of each object to the nearest quarter-inch.

1.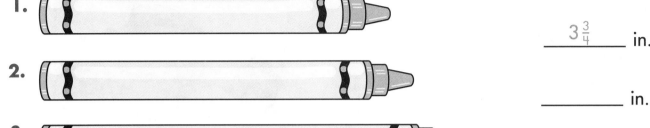

_____ $3\frac{3}{4}$ _____ in.

2.

_____ in.

3.

_____ in.

4.

_____ in.

5.

_____ in.

6.

_____ in.

7.

_____ in.

8.

_____ in.

9.

_____ in.

Use the information above to fill in the line plot.

Crayons Used in the Classroom (in.)

10.

$3\frac{3}{4}$ 4 $4\frac{1}{4}$ $4\frac{1}{2}$ $4\frac{3}{4}$

Lesson 7.4 Gathering Data to Draw a Line Plot

Use a ruler to measure the length of each object to the nearest quarter-inch.

1.

$1\frac{3}{4}$

_____ in.

2.

_____ in.

4.

_____ in.

3.

_____ in.

5.

_____ in.

6.

_____ in.

7.

_____ in.

Use the information above to fill in the line plot.

8.

Fish in the Pond (in.)

$1\frac{1}{2}$ $1\frac{3}{4}$ 2 $2\frac{1}{4}$ $2\frac{1}{2}$

Lesson 7.5 Finding Area with Unit Squares

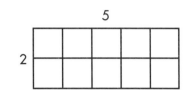

A = 1 square unit   A = ___10___ sq. units   A = ___4___ sq. cm

Find the area.

a   **b**

1.
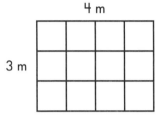

4 m

3 m

A = _____ sq. m

2.
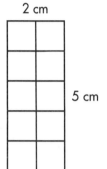

2 cm

5 cm

A = _____ sq. cm

3.
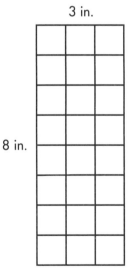

3 in.

8 in.

A = _____ sq. in.

4.

7 m

4 m

A = _____ sq. m

5.
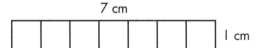

7 cm

1 cm

A = _____ sq. cm

6.
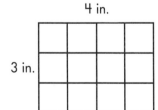

4 in.

3 in.

A = _____ sq. in.

Lesson 7.5 Finding Area with Unit Squares

3 in.

6 in.

Find the area by drawing
the square units.

Count the square units to
find the area.

Draw 5 lines across to
make 6 rows.

6 in.

3 in.

6 in.

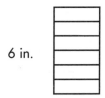

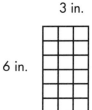

Draw 2 lines down to
make 3 columns.

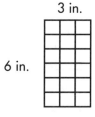

3 in.

6 in.

A = ____18____ sq. in.

Draw the square units to find the area.

1. 4 cm

2 cm

A = _____ sq. cm

2. 4 cm

7 cm

A = _____ sq. cm

3. 3 in.

3 in.

A = _____ sq. in.

4. 3 m

1 m

A = _____ sq. m

5. 2 cm

2 cm

A = _____ sq. cm

6. 1 cm

5 cm

A = _____ sq. cm

Lesson 7.9 Measuring Perimeter

Perimeter is the distance around a shape.

To calculate perimeter, add together the lengths of all the sides.

Perimeter = 17 in. + 10 in. + 17 in. + 10 in.

Perimeter = 54 in.

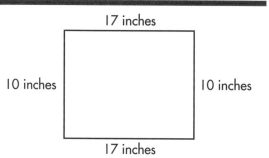

17 inches

10 inches   10 inches

17 inches

Find the perimeter of each shape.

a	b	c

1.

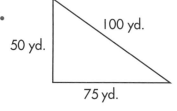

3 yd.

4 yd.   4 yd.

3 yd.

_____ yd.

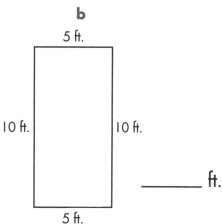

5 ft.

10 ft.   10 ft.

5 ft.

_____ ft.

13 in.   13 in.

2 in.

_____ in.

2.

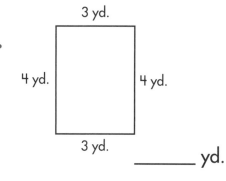

50 yd.   100 yd.

75 yd.

_____ yd.

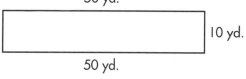

50 yd.

10 yd.   10 yd.

50 yd.

_____ yd.

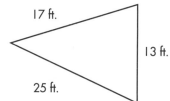

17 ft.

13 ft.

25 ft.

_____ ft.

Find the unknown side.

3.

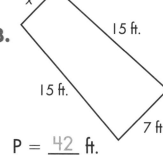

x

15 ft.

15 ft.

7 ft.

P = _42_ ft.

x = ___ ft.

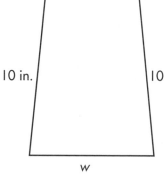

6 in.

10 in.   10 in.

w

P = _34_ in.

w = ___ in.

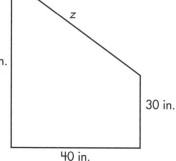

60 in.

z

30 in.

40 in.

P = _160_ in.

z = ___ in.

Lesson 7.9 Problem Solving

SHOW YOUR WORK

Solve.

1. The town of Yarmouth is planning a skateboard park and needs to know the perimeter of the park. The property measures __ yards by 3 yards by 10 yards by 5 yards. What is the perimeter?

   The park's perimeter is _____ yards.

2. John cleared a vacant lot to plant a garden. The lot measured 55 by 15 feet. What is the perimeter of the garden lot?

   The perimeter of the lot is _____ feet.

3. Gabriel built a cage for his tropical birds. The cage measures 14 feet by 12 feet. What is the perimeter of the cage?

   The perimeter of the cage is _____ feet.

4. The length of the walking track is 103 feet and the width is 50 feet. What is the perimeter of the track?

   The perimeter is _____ feet.

5. Anna is buying trim to go around her rug. Her rug measures 54 inches by 42 inches. How many inches of trim will Anna need to buy?

   Anna will need to buy _____ inches of trim.

6. Natalie is putting a fence around her pool. Her pool is 10 feet by 8 feet. How many feet of fencing will Natalie need?

   Natalie will need _____ feet of fencing.

7. The rectangular third-grade classroom has a perimeter of 130 feet. If it is 25 feet wide, how many feet long is the classroom?

   The classroom is _____ feet long.

| 1. |
| 2. |
| 3. |
| 4. |
| 5. |
| 6. |
| 7. |

Check What You Learned

Measurement

Choose an answer.

a	b
1. About how much does a paper clip weigh?	About how much juice can a baby bottle hold?

a. 1 gram

b. 100 grams

c. 1,000 grams

a. 3 liters

b. 30 milliliters

c. 300 liters

Solve.

2. Kennedy popped 24 cups of popcorn in 3 days. If she popped the same number of cups each day, how many cups did she pop each day?

_____

Complete the graphs.

a

b

3.

Miles Canoed
Team 1 = 60
Team 2 = 40
Team 3 = 140

Favorite Pets
Gerbil = 4
Goldfish = 3
Iguana = 1

Miles Canoed	

Key _____ = 20 miles

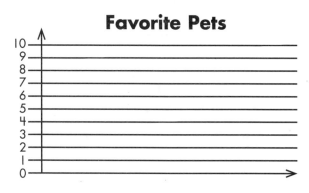

Favorite Pets

Check What You Learned

Measurement

Find the area of the figure.

a	b

4.

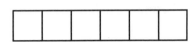

_____ sq. units   _____ sq. units

---

5. Draw the square units to show the area of the rectangle.

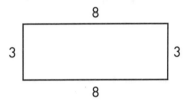

A = _____ sq. units

6. Multiply to find the area.

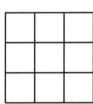

A = _____ sq. in.

---

7. Find the area.

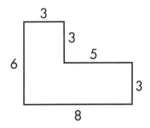

A = _____ sq. units

8. Solve.

An equilateral triangle has one side that measures 9 cm. How many centimeters is the perimeter of the triangle?

_____

Check What You Know

Time

Complete the following.

	a	b
1.	2:32 means ___ minutes after ___.	2:32 means ___ minutes to ___.
2.	3:45 means ___ minutes after ___.	3:45 means ___ minutes to ___.
3.	9:50 means ___ minutes after ___.	9:50 means ___ minutes to ___.

Tell the time to the nearest hour, half hour, quarter hour, or minute as indicated.

4.

a	b	c	d
hour	half hour	quarter hour	minute
___ : ___	___ : ___	___ : ___	___ : ___

Solve.

a

5. Carrie's family leaves at 7:15 p.m. They drive for 30 minutes and then stop for dinner. What time is it when they stop?

_____

b

Look at the clock. Blair arrived at the bus stop 45 minutes ago. What time did Blair arrive at the bus stop?

_____

Solve. Use the number line to show how much time has elapsed.

6. Blane left work at 2:15 p.m. He ate dinner at 7:15 p.m. How much time passed between the time Blane left work and ate dinner?

_____

2:15 p.m.   7:15 p.m.

├──┤

Lesson 8.1 Telling Time

 5:15 is read "five fifteen" and means "15 minutes after 5."

 12:50 is read "twelve fifty" and means "50 minutes after 12" or "10 minutes to 1."

 4:45 is read "four forty-five" and means "45 minutes after 4," or "15 minutes to 5."

Complete the following.

	a	b
1.	6:15 means __15__ minutes after __6__.	11:50 means ____ minutes to ____.
2.	7:50 means ____ minutes after ____.	7:50 means ____ minutes to ____.
3.	12:45 means ____ minutes after ____.	12:45 means ____ minutes to ____.
4.	1:30 means ____ minutes after ____.	1:30 means ____ minutes to ____.

For each analog clock face, write the numerals that name the time.

a   b   c   d

5.

___ : ___   ___ : ___   ___ : ___   ___ : ___

6.

___ : ___   ___ : ___   ___ : ___   ___ : ___

Lesson 8.1 Telling Time

6:41

The closest hour on an analog clock is determined by the hour hand (the short hand).

The closest half hour, quarter hour, and minute are determined by the minute hand (the long hand).

A half hour is at 30 minutes or 1 hour.

A quarter hour is at 15, 30, 45 minutes, or 1 hour.

What time is it to the nearest hour? ___7:00___, half hour? ___6:30___,

quarter hour? ___6:45___, minute? ___6:41___

Write the time to the nearest hour, half hour, quarter hour, or minute as indicated.

	a	b	c	d
1. 	hour ___ : ___	half hour ___ : ___	quarter hour ___ : ___	minute ___ : ___
2. 	hour ___ : ___	half hour ___ : ___	quarter hour ___ : ___	minute ___ : ___

Draw the hands on the analog clock to express the time presented on the digital clock.

a   b

3. 3:15   7:32

4. 12:07   2:00

Lesson 8.2 Time on a Number Line

Quinn gets up at 7:30 a.m. She leaves the house at 9:20 a.m. How much time passed between when she got up and left the house?

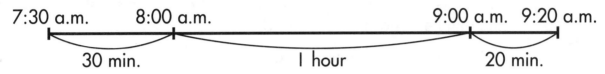

| 7:30 a.m. | 8:00 a.m. | | 9:00 a.m. 9:20 a.m. |
| 30 min. | 1 hour | | 20 min. |

First, find out how much time until the next hour.
Second, find out how much time passed since the previous hour.
Then, find out how much time passed between the next hour and the previous hour.
Last, add up the minutes and hours to find out the total time that has passed.

_____ 1 hour 50 minutes _____

Solve.

1. Alexa went to the bookstore at 5:45 p.m. She left the bookstore at 9:10 p.m. How long was Alexa at the bookstore?

_____

5:45 p.m.   9:10 p.m.

2. Hugo leaves for work at 7:45 a.m. He leaves work to go home at 4:15 p.m. How much time does Hugo spend at work?

_____

7:45 a.m.   4:15 p.m.

Check What You Learned

 Time

Complete the following.

a	b

1. 4:15 means ___ minutes after ___.   4:15 means ___ minutes to ___.

2. 12:55 means ___ minutes after ___.   12:55 means ___ minutes to ___.

3. 6:40 means ___ minutes after ___.   6:40 means ___ minutes to ___.

Tell the time to the nearest hour, half hour, quarter hour, or minute as indicated.

4.

a	b	c	d
hour	half hour	quarter hour	minute
___ : ___	___ : ___	___ : ___	___ : ___

Solve. Show the elapsed time on the number line.

5. Fiona takes her puppy to the park at 8:40 a.m. She goes to the lake, then to a friend's house, and gets home at 12:10 p.m. How much time was Fiona out of the house?

_____

8:40 a.m.   12:10 p.m.

6. Jonathan goes to school at 8:50 a.m. The last bell rings at 3:05 p.m. How much time is Jonathan at school?

_____

8:50 a.m.   3:05 p.m.

NAME _____

Check What You Know

Geometry

1. Divide the circle into fourths. Label each fourth with the appropriate fraction.

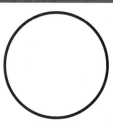

2. Divide the square into thirds. Label each third with the appropriate fraction.

3. Divide the rectangle into sixths. Label each sixth with the appropriate fraction.

Complete each table.

	Figure	Number of Sides	Number of Square Corners	Number of Other Corners		Figure	Number of Square Faces	Number of Triangle Faces	Number of Rectangle Faces	Number of Edges
4.	square				**7.**	cube				
5.	circle				**8.**	square pyramid				
6.	rectangle				**9.**	sphere				

Circle the shapes named.

10. Circle the quadrilaterals.

11. Circle the rectangles.

12. Circle the rhombuses.

Lesson 9.1 Plane Figures

A **plane figure** is a flat surface.

circle   triangle   square   rectangle

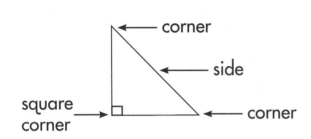

Each side of a triangle, square, and rectangle is a **line segment**.

The point where two line segments meet is a **corner** or a **square corner**.

A square corner is a right angle. A right angle has a measure of 90°.

Draw the following plane figures.

	a	b	c	d
1.	triangle	rectangle	square	circle

Complete the following.

	a	b	c	d	e
2. number of sides	0				
3. number of square corners			1		0
4. number of other corners					

Lesson 9.2 Solid Figures

A **solid figure** is a three-dimensional object. Solid figures may be hollow or solid.

 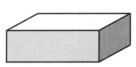

cube   rectangular   square   sphere   cylinder   cone
            prism   pyramid

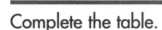

square
corner

corner

face

edge

corner

face

edge

A **face** is the shape formed by the edges of a solid figure.

An **edge** is where 2 faces intersect.

A **vertex** or **corner** is the point where 3 or more edges come together.

Complete the table.

	Solid Figure	Number of Square Faces	Number of Rectangle Faces	Number of Triangle Faces
I.	cube			0
2.	rectangular prism			
3.	square pyramid	1		

4. How many edges does a sphere have? _____ edges

5. How many edges does a square pyramid have? _____ edges

6. How many edges does a cube have? _____ edges

7. How many edges does a rectangular prism have? _____ edges

8. How many corners does a square pyramid have? _____ corners

Give a physical example of each of the following plane figures.

	a	**b**	**c**
9.	cube	rectangular prism	square pyramid
	sugar cube		
10.	sphere	cylinder	cone

Lesson 9.3 Classifying Quadrilaterals

Quadrilaterals are four-sided shapes. To be a quadrilateral, all four sides must be connected.

Parallelograms are quadrilaterals with two sets of parallel sides.

Rectangles are parallelograms with four right angles.

Rhombuses are parallelograms with four sides of equal length.

Squares are rectangles with four equal sides. They are also rhombuses with four right angles.

Circle the shapes named. Then, answer the question.

1. Circle the quadrilaterals.

2. Circle the parallelograms.

3. Circle the rectangles.

4. Circle the rhombuses.

5. Circle the squares.

6. Which of the shapes defined above fits into all five categories?

_____

Lesson 9.4 Dividing Shapes

Halves = 2 equal pieces

Thirds = 3 equal pieces

Fourths = 4 equal pieces

Fifths = 5 equal pieces

and so on . . .

Divide this shape into thirds.

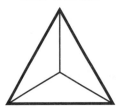

Label each third.

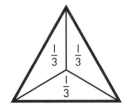

Divide each shape into the given amount of equal parts. Then, label each piece with the appropriate fraction.

1. halves

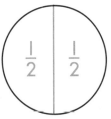

2. thirds

3. thirds

4. halves

5. fourths

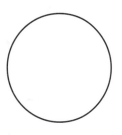

6. fifths

7. halves

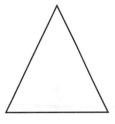

8. fourths

Check What You Learned

Geometry

Divide each shape into the given amount of equal parts. Then, label each piece with the appropriate fraction.

a   **b**

1. fifths 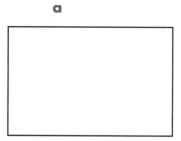   thirds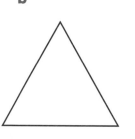

2. halves    fourths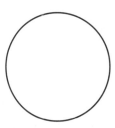

Name each four-sided figure.

       a   **b**   **c**   **d**

3.    

_____   _____   _____   _____

How many sides or edges are there on these figures?

       a   **b**   **c**   **d**

4.

_____   _____   _____   _____

NAME _____

 Check What You Know

Preparing for Algebra

Complete the pattern by using addition or subtraction.

				a	b	c	d
1.	30	26	22	____	____	____	____
2.	1	2	3	____	____	____	____
3.	5	10	15	____	____	____	____
4.	4	8	16	____	____	____	____
5.	1	3	5	____	____	____	____
6.	10	9	8	____	____	____	____

Write the number sentence. For the missing part, use a box (☐). Solve each number sentence.

7. Thirty-six divided by a number equals six. _____

The number is _____.

8. The product of five and four equals what number? _____

The product of five and four is _____.

9. This number divided by three equals seven. _____

This number is _____.

10. This number times four equals twenty-four. _____

This number is _____.

11. Thirty-five divided by five equals what number? _____

Fourteen divided by 5 is _____.

12. The product of nine and this number equals eighteen. _____

This number is _____.

13. This number divided by three equals six. _____

This number is _____.

Lesson 10.2 Number Sentences

A **number sentence** is an equation with numbers.

Identity Property	**Commutative Property**
for addition: $0 + 3 = 3$	for addition: $3 + 2 = 2 + 3$
for multiplication: $1 \times 3 = 3$	for multiplication: $4 \times 2 = 2 \times 4$

A number sentence can change its look but not change its value.

$3 + 5 = 8$ or $3 + 5 = 4 + 4$ $\qquad$ $3 \times 8 = 24$ or $3 \times 8 = 6 \times 4$

Complete each number sentence.

	a	b	c	d
1.	$0 + 4 = \boxed{4}$	$0 + 6 = \square$	$\square + 2 = 2$	$\square + 7 = 7$
2.	$1 \times 2 = \square$	$1 \times 5 = \square$	$\square \times 4 = 4$	$\square \times 9 = 9$
3.	$7 + 2 = \square + 7$	$3 + 4 = \square + 3$	$1 + 2 = 2 + \square$	$\square + 5 = 5 + 4$
4.	$5 \times 7 = 7 \times \square$	$4 \times \square = 3 \times 4$	$\square \times 3 = 3 \times 5$	$9 \times 4 = \square \times 9$

Complete the following.

	a	b	c	d
5.	$2 + 7 = 9$ or $2 + 7 = 5 + \boxed{4}$	$5 + 7 = 12$ or $5 + 7 = 6 + \square$	$4 + 3 = 7$ or $4 + 3 = 5 + \square$	$6 + 9 = 15$ or $6 + 9 = 10 + \square$
6.	$6 + 4 = 10$ or $6 + 4 = 5 + \square$	$6 + 7 = 13$ or $6 + 7 = 8 + \square$	$5 + 3 = 8$ or $5 + 3 = 6 + \square$	$9 + 2 = 11$ or $9 + 2 = 5 + \square$
7.	$5 \times 6 = 30$ or $5 \times 6 = 10 \times \square$	$4 \times 3 = 12$ or $4 \times 3 = 2 \times \square$	$6 \times 3 = 18$ or $6 \times 3 = 9 \times \square$	$6 \times 2 = 12$ or $6 \times 2 = 4 \times \square$

Lesson 10.2 Number Sentences

Associative Property	**Distributive Property**

Associative Property:

$2 \times 3 \times 4 = c$

$2 \times 3 = 6$

$6 \times 4 = 24$

$c = 24$

Distributive Property:

$6 + 5 = 11$

$11 \times 8 = (6 \times 8) + (5 \times 8)$

$48 + 40 = 88$

$11 \times 8 = 88$

Solve using the associative property.

	a	**b**

1. $2 \times 3 \times 5 = d$ $1 \times 2 \times 9 = h$

_____ × _____ = _____   _____ × _____ = _____

_____ × _____ = _____   _____ × _____ = _____

$d =$ _____ $h =$ _____

2. $2 \times 4 \times 6 = e$ $2 \times 4 \times 7 = g$

_____ × _____ = _____   _____ × _____ = _____

_____ × _____ = _____   _____ × _____ = _____

$e =$ _____ $g =$ _____

Solve using the distributive property.

3. $12 \times 4 = (10 \times 4) + ($____ $\times 4)$ $14 \times 3 = (10 \times 3) + ($____ $\times 3)$

____ + ____   ____ + ____

$12 \times 4 =$ ____ $14 \times 3 =$ ____

4. $19 \times 2 = (10 \times 2) + ($____ $\times 2)$ $16 \times 5 = (10 \times 5) + ($____ $\times 5)$

____ + ____   ____ + ____

$19 \times 2 =$ ____ $16 \times 5 =$ ____

Lesson 10.2 Problem Solving

Math Symbol	Key Words
=	is, is equal to, equals
+	added to, sum, and, plus
−	subtracted from, difference, minus
×	multiplied by, the product of, times
÷	divided by

Write each number sentence. Put a box (☐) in the sentence for the missing part. Solve each number sentence.

1. The sum of two and three is what number? $2 + 3 = \boxed{5}$

   The sum of two and three is ____five____.

2. Seven minus two is what number? _____

   Seven minus two is _____.

3. Four times three is what number? _____

   Four times three is _____.

4. Fourteen divided by two is what number? _____

   Fourteen divided by two is _____.

5. Five added to what number is seven? _____

   Five added to _____ is seven.

6. Thirteen minus what number is ten? _____

   Thirteen minus _____ is ten.

Lesson 10.2 Problem Solving

Write each number sentence. Put a box (☐) in the sentence for the missing part.
Solve each number sentence.

1. Twenty-seven divided by a number equals three. _____

   Twenty-seven divided by _____ equals three.

2. This number divided by eight equals eight. _____

   _____ divided by eight equals eight.

3. Twelve divided by three equals what number? _____

   Twelve divided by three equals _____

4. Four times nine is what number? _____

   Four times nine is _____.

5. This number times eight is fifty-six. _____

   _____ times eight is fifty-six.

6. Nine times this number is eighty-one. _____

   Nine times _____ is eighty-one.

7. Twenty divided by four is what number? _____

   Twenty divided by four is _____.

8. Ten times this number is ninety. _____

   Ten times _____ is ninety.

9. This number times five is twenty-five. _____

   _____ times five is twenty-five.

10. This number divided by seven is nine. _____

    _____ divided by seven is nine.

Check What You Learned

Preparing for Algebra

Complete the pattern by using addition or subtraction.

				a	b	c	d
1.	1	2	3	____	____	____	____
2.	50	45	40	____	____	____	____
3.	100	90	80	____	____	____	____
4.	4	8	12	____	____	____	____
5.	2	4	6	____	____	____	____
6.	33	35	37	____	____	____	____

Write the number sentence. For the missing part, use a box (☐). Solve each number sentence.

7. Twelve divided by six is what number? _____

Twelve divided by six is _____.

8. Seven times three is what number? _____

Seven times three is _____.

9. Five plus six is what number? _____

Five plus six is _____.

10. This number divided by four equals eight. _____

_____ divided by four equals eight.

11. Nine times this number equals seventy-two. _____

Nine times _____ equals seventy-two.

12. Twelve times five equals what number? _____

Twelve times five equals _____.

Check What You Learned

Preparing for Algebra

Complete the following.

	a	b	c	d
13.	$5 + \square = 5$	$\square + 0 = 4$	$2 \times 1 = \square$	$3 \times 1 = \square$
14.	$2 + 7 = 9$ or	$5 + 9 = 14$ or	$3 \times 8 = 24$ or	$6 \times 2 = 12$ or
	$2 + 7 = 6 + \square$	$5 + 9 = 8 + \square$	$3 \times 8 = 4 \times \square$	$6 \times 2 = 4 \times \square$

Complete the following.

a

15. $3 \times 2 \times 3 = y$

$3 \times 2 = 6$

$6 \times 3 =$ _____

$y =$ _____

b

$4 \times 1 \times 2 = z$

$4 \times 1 = 4$

$4 \times 2 =$ _____

$z =$ _____

c

$2 \times 3 \times 6 = m$

$2 \times 3 = 6$

$6 \times 6 =$ _____

$m =$ _____

16. $2 \times 3 \times 8 = a$

_____ × _____ = _____

_____ × _____ = _____

$a =$ _____

$1 \times 2 \times 7 = c$

_____ × _____ = _____

_____ × _____ = _____

$c =$ _____

$1 \times 5 \times 6 = k$

_____ × _____ = _____

_____ × _____ = _____

$k =$ _____

Complete the following.

17. $13 \times 7 = (10 \times 7) + ($_____ $\times 7)$

_____ + _____ = _____

18. $16 \times 6 = (10 \times 6) + ($_____ $\times 6)$

_____ + _____ = _____

19. $18 \times 4 = (10 \times 4) + ($_____ $\times 4)$

_____ + _____ = _____

Final Test Chapters 1–10

What fraction of each figure or set is shaded?

 a    b   c   d

16.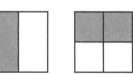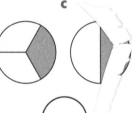

_____   _____   _____   _____

What fraction of each figure is shaded? Compare the fractions. Use >, <, or =.

a   b   c

17.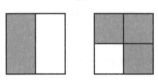

____ ◯ ____   ____ ◯ ____   ____ ◯ ____

18.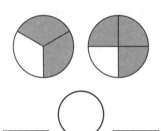

____ ◯ ____   ____ ◯ ____   ____ ◯ ____

Label the fractions on the number line.

19. $\frac{3}{4}$

20. $\frac{2}{3}$

Complete the fractions.

21.   = ____   **22.**   = ____

Final Test Chapters 1–10

Choose an answer.

a	**b**

23. About how much does a baby weigh?

  a. 8 ounces

  b. 8 pounds

  c. 8 gallons

About how much milk does a jug hold?

  a. 1 gram

  b. 1 gallon

  c. 1 kilogram

Solve each problem.

24. Baby Ginny weighs 9 pounds. Baby Tyler weighs 13 pounds. How much do the babies weigh altogether?

The babies weigh _____ pounds altogether.

Find the area of each figure.

a	**b**	**c**

25.

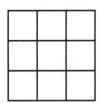

A = _____ sq. units

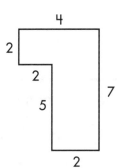

A = _____ sq. units   A = _____ sq. units

Solve.

26. Roxanne is fencing a garden. Two sides of the garden are 18 feet, and the other two are 12 feet. How many feet of fencing will Roxanne need?

Roxanne will need _____ feet of fencing.

Final Test Chapters 1–10

Complete the bar graph.

27.

Sea Animals Observed
Starfish = 5
Clams = 4
Dolphins = 2

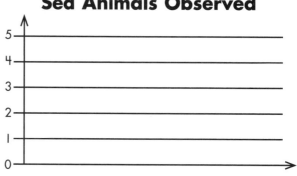

Sea Animals Observed

Complete the following.

	a		b

28. 7:42 means ___ minutes after ___.   7:42 means ___ minutes to ___.

Write the time to the nearest hour, half hour, quarter hour, or minute as indicated.

29.

a	b	c	d
hour	half hour	quarter hour	minute
___ : ___	___ : ___	___ : ___	___ : ___

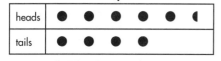

Coin Flip Results

heads	● ● ● ● ● ◖
tails	● ● ● ●

Key: ● = 2 students

Use this picture graph to answer the following questions.

30. How many students flipped heads? _____

31. How many students flipped tails? _____

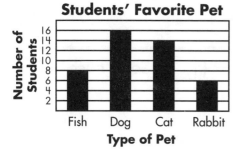

Students' Favorite Pet

Use this bar graph to answer the following questions.

32. Which pet did the most students choose?

_____

33. Which pet did the fewest students choose?

_____

Spectrum Math
Grade 3

Final Test Chapters 1–10

Name each figure. Label each as solid or plane.

| a | b | c | d |

34.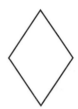

_____   _____   _____   _____

_____   _____   _____   _____

Name each four-sided figure.

35.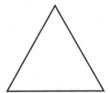

_____   _____   _____   _____

Divide each shape into the given fractional parts. Then, label each piece with an appropriate fraction.

36. halves ᵃ   fourths ᵇ   thirds ᶜ

Complete the patterns.

| | | | a | b | | | | c | d |

37.   20   25   30   ___   ___   13   11   9   ___   ___

Complete the following.

| a | b | c | d |

38. $3 + 0 = \square$ $5 \times 1 = \square$ $5 + 3 = \square + 5$ $7 \times 2 = 2 \times \square$

Write the number sentence. For the missing part, use a box ($\square$). Solve each number sentence.

39. The product of five and two is what number? _____

The product of five and two is _____.

Scoring Record for Posttests, Mid-Test, and Final Test

Chapter Posttest	Your Score	Performance			
		Excellent	Very Good	Fair	Needs Improvement
1	____ of 54	51–54	44–50	33–43	32 or fewer
2	____ of 54	51–54	44–50	33–43	32 or fewer
3	____ of 39	37–39	32–36	23–31	22 or fewer
4	____ of 59	56–59	48–55	36–47	35 or fewer
5	____ of 51	48–51	42–47	32–41	31 or fewer
6	____ of 16	15–16	13–14	11–12	11 or fewer
7	____ of 11	11	9–10	6–8	5 or fewer
8	____ of 12	12	10–11	7–9	6 or fewer
9	____ of 12	12	10–11	7–9	6 or fewer
10	____ of 47	44–47	38–43	28–37	27 or fewer
Mid-Test	____ of 93	87–93	75–86	56–74	55 or fewer
Final Test	____ of 110	103–110	89–102	67–88	66 or fewer

Record your test score in the Your Score column. See where your score falls in the Performance columns. Your score is based on the total number of required responses. If your score is fair or needs improvement, review the chapter material.

Grade 3 Answers

Chapter 1

Pretest, page 5

	a	b	c	d	e
1.	42	22	79	86	90
2.	19	94	57	81	70
3.	53	32	45	43	95
4.	99	94	53	93	88
5.	80	7	5	20	8
6.	41	61	5	20	43
7.	39	23	54	35	65
8.	8	61	35	50	15

Pretest, page 6

9. 63; 27; 36 **10.** 43; 13; 16; 72
11. 36; 22; 14 **12.** 25

Lesson 1.1, page 7

	a	b	c	d	e	f
1.	5	16	7	8	3	14
2.	9	6	9	11	7	13
3.	7	11	14	11	14	6
4.	0	11	14	7	8	12
5.	7	4	6	10	16	9
6.	9	12	12	15	18	12

Lesson 1.2, page 8

	a	b	c	d	e	f
1.	5	6	1	5	7	5
2.	3	3	3	8	9	2
3.	5	3	6	3	7	7
4.	11	1	8	8	5	13
5.	7	2	1	9	4	6
6.	2	6	8	4	1	6

Lesson 1.3, page 9

	a	b	c	d	e	f
1.	39	33	30	28	88	76
2.	27	48	27	83	92	55
3.	26	47	59	80	77	44
4.	59	55	56	48	69	69
5.	27	58	65	93	97	58
6.	53	93	99	65	68	77

Lesson 1.4, page 10

	a	b	c	d	e	f
1.	11	64	22	20	81	32
2.	52	70	21	42	12	56
3.	41	22	27	13	44	30
4.	41	21	12	22	21	12
5.	30	21	11	54	21	16
6.	10	16	23	31	61	41

Lesson 1.5, page 11

	a	b	c	d	e	f
1.	41	91	90	52	81	48
2.	63	91	64	80	83	72
3.	81	81	45	32	56	70
4.	81	45	81	31	90	54
5.	80	45	41	52	54	91
6.	46	61	70	51	60	91

Lesson 1.6, page 12

	a	b	c	d	e	f
1.	8	3	25	14	36	59
2.	17	6	34	19	17	19
3.	35	15	46	29	25	24
4.	7	40	59	67	35	19
5.	48	27	23	57	36	19
6.	36	47	68	55	18	39

Lesson 1.7, page 13

	a	b	c	d	e	f
1.	84	92	64	68	48	90
2.	98	72	60	53	71	84
3.	83	52	19	91	74	85
4.	96	92	93	66	91	89

5. 95 68 91 55 58 75

Lesson 1.8, page 14

	a	b	c	d	e	f
1.	13	97	63	36	51	46
2.	70	17	52	33	42	13
3.	84	79	75	87	8	72
4.	67	93	14	23	40	47
5.	14	18	30	19	73	71
6.	2	61	99	56	13	91

Lesson 1.9, page 15

1. 52; 39; 91 **2.** 3; 23; 2; 28
3. 27; 31; 58 **4.** 53 **5.** 90

Lesson 1.10, page 16

1. 32; 14; 18 **2.** 15; 11; 4 **3.** 76; 62; 14
4. 17 **5.** 26

Posttest, page 17

	a	b	c	d	e	f
1.	70	39	71	33	80	27
2.	98	92	50	70	48	84
3.	60	36	20	75	77	99
4.	91	81	48	90	66	59
5.	88	63	37	26	2	63
6.	68	15	23	22	49	14
7.	23	60	56	47	64	67
8.	8	16	72	45	40	25

Posttest, page 18

9. 17 **10.** 38 **11.** 19 **12.** 16 **13.** 8
14. 17

Chapter 2

Pretest, page 19

	a	b	c	d	e	f
1.	70	178	182	95	199	283
2.	792	979	420	905	369	160

3. 228 277 208 169 77 417
4. 80 121 818 967 599 68
5. 108 64 510 16 94 639
6. 444 442 848 602 732 40
7. 35 52 37 61 609 426
8. 810 44 65 430 534 137

Pretest, page 20

9. subtract; 14 **10.** add; 81 **11.** add; 73
12. 107 **13.** 204

Lesson 2.1, page 21

	a	b	c	d	e	f
1.	118	103	140	118	110	162
2.	94	119	105	113	158	114
3.	102	119	161	115	127	121
4.	114	104	119	102	105	170
5.	100	107	120	111	139	86
6.	139	187	150	118	126	139

Lesson 2.1, page 22

1. 58; 47; 105 **2.** 72; 43; 115
3. 92; 87;179 **4.** 77; 52; 129

Lesson 2.2, page 23

	a	b	c	d	e	f
1.	140	61	151	111	94	92
2.	81	110	104	111	121	145
3.	141	44	120	93	91	111
4.	81	134	121	94	62	80
5.	43	101	80	141	127	92
6.	114	122	120	94	88	77
7.	93	124	92	70	122	71

Lesson 2.2, page 24

	a	b	c	d	e	f
1.	89	78	88	86	77	39
2.	79	79	67	66	68	86

3.	26	8	48	89	69	88
4.	78	58	69	86	59	76
5.	28	58	29	58	74	87
6.	85	69	79	75	87	58
7.	79	89	57	88	78	87

Lesson 2.2, page 25

	a	b	c	d	e	f
1.	61	109	106	92	90	31
2.	55	71	84	59	117	111
3.	80	70	105	47	74	78
4.	91	91	97	66	72	81
5.	91	67	129	85	89	89
6.	87	89	101	98	71	113
7.	58	91	116	82	79	94
8.	84	64	122	115	124	87
9.	7	78	78	49	91	87

Lesson 2.2, page 26

1. 119; 57; 62 **2.** 162; 54; 108
3. 117; 59; 58 **4.** 153; 62; 91

Lesson 2.3, page 27

	a	b	c	d	e	f
1.	685	1,153	933	1,123	444	1,656
2.	1,175	1,030	1,570	1,042	1,280	868
3.	1,282	1,001	681	973	1,356	1,194
4.	982	944	367	404	414	1,234
5.	1,424	850	1,378	1,350	446	812
6.	1,334	1,070	880	1,251	1,125	839
7.	465	922	1,334	521	967	874

Lesson 2.3, page 28

1. 232; 179; 411 **2.** 543; 476; 1,019
3. 639; 722; 1,361 **4.** 324; 187; 511

Lesson 2.4, page 29

	a	b	c	d	e	f
1.	212	593	489	120	480	148
2.	408	206	279	106	377	190
3.	331	399	519	189	577	321
4.	114	208	529	171	448	220
5.	86	627	25	350	86	838
6.	281	349	225	336	129	485

Lesson 2.4, page 30

1. 990; 587; 403 **2.** 530; 147; 383
3. 600; 230; 370 **4.** 171 **5.** 197

Lesson 2.5, page 31

	a	b	c	d	e	f
1.	369	901	417	732	521	290
2.	1,108	606	1,075	1,005	397	476
3.	847	711	931	550	531	506
4.	1,055	589	812	902	382	695

Lesson 2.6, page 32

	a	b	c	d	e	f
1.	570	238	33	326	165	222
2.	121	15	226	112	129	296
3.	399	220	106	263	264	405
4.	187	462	437	303	215	198

Lesson 2.7, page 33

	a	b	c	d	e	f
1.	131	179	91	94	422	214
2.	268	62	337	60	779	60
3.	447	77	89	175	198	99
4.	1,403	313	860	79	465	769
5.	905	365	370	198	204	915
6.	223	922	689	396	302	93
7.	75	119	120	649	905	293
8.	106	585	349	91	402	344
9.	1,344	118	390	580	149	628

Grade 3 Answers

Lesson 2.7, page 34

	a	b	c	d	e	f
1.	131	158	86	117	664	640
2.	401	162	520	140	197	102
3.	1,111	164	620	999	329	716
4.	397	108	183	409	889	105
5.	88	147	591	430	406	206
6.	306	463	378	106	403	631
7.	677	728	582	928	272	142
8.	256	459	93	452	96	930
9.	340	120	455	241	239	243

Posttest, page 35

	a	b	c	d	e	f
1.	167	345	249	402	922	868
2.	279	375	1,750	345	1,273	360
3.	969	407	856	1,042	915	990
4.	829	715	1,029	527	725	1,010
5.	137	106	78	40	270	186
6.	288	617	231	115	394	364
7.	159	477	187	683	485	169
8.	310	335	224	478	341	107

Posttest, page 36

9. 6 **10.** 8 **11.** 219 **12.** 1,223
13. 28 **14.** 76

Chapter 3

Pretest, page 37

	a	b	c	d	e
1.	39	162	62	22	126
2.	961	730	1,308	1,444	1,691
3.	6,556	9,315	6,796	7,162	9,971
4.	960	1,540	380	3,340	3,881
5.	1,675	3,811	733	1,117	830
6.	2,822	292	391	300	3,780
7.	540	900	480	1,000	

Pretest, page 38

8. 11 **9.** 205 **10.** 1,759 **11.** 2,802
12. 100 − 60 = 40 **13.** 40 + 30 = 70

Lesson 3.1, page 39

	a	b	c	d	e	f
1.	18	20	31	44	97	16
2.	133	153	123	83	142	150
3.	251	120	120	223	157	55
4.	163	183	188	39	120	212
5.	224	202	215	73	181	202

Lesson 3.1, page 40

1. 23; 16; 14; 7; 60 **2.** 9; 6; 7; 22
3. 53; 44; 18; 115 **4.** 25

Lesson 3.2, page 41

	a	b	c	d	e	f
1.	1,040	1,594	650	1,794	1,616	914
2.	1,612	973	2,417	445	1,100	723
3.	2,027	2,158	1,489	1,673	1,239	1,867
4.	660	1,612	1,285	1,279	1,802	1,353
5.	2,533	1,487	1,980	525	1,774	2,280

Lesson 3.2, page 42

1. 135; 213; 159; 507
2. 186; 175; 182; 543 **3.** 2,325 **4.** 442

Lesson 3.3, page 43

	a	b	c	d	e	f
1.	9,057	9,873	7,389	7,464	9,469	9,803
2.	3,764	9,990	9,311	7,296	9,793	8,052
3.	7,757	9,281	8,405	4,065	9,173	8,485
4.	8,420	9,465	3,578	8,874	9,717	9,512
5.	7,413	9,232	5,532	9,044	9,768	6,708
6.	7,437	7,309	6,858	9,914	9,292	9,905

Grade 3 Answers

Lesson 3.3, page 44
1. 1,523; 1,695; 3,218
2. 1,200; 1,320; 2,520 3. 2,122 4. 2,600

Lesson 3.4, page 45

	a	b	c	d	e
1.	7,483	6,736	4,661	1,742	894
2.	1,882	8,080	6,982	7,882	3,872
3.	4,092	595	1,582	5,291	7,481
4.	6,891	2,795	7,492	3,493	2,791
5.	8,891	2,893	1,781	2,892	7,641
6.	4,672	3,480	6,891	3,294	4,573

Lesson 3.4, page 46
1. 2,532; 1,341; 1,191
2. 1,250; 495; 755
3. 1,986; 103; 1,883 4. 54 5. 191

Lesson 3.5, page 47

	a	b	c	d
1.	960	150	190	4,030
2.	130	3,450	8,660	7,990
3.	8,800	1,000	3,300	7,900
4.	500	1,300	800	4,400
5.	8,600	1,900	360	1,540
6.	1,900	770	900	90
7.	450	8,710	500	5,330
8.	3,700	120	490	2,400

Lesson 3.5, page 48

	a	b	c	d
1.	540	900	480	960
2.	5,700	9,650	4,400	1,610
3.	600	90	5,400	980
4.	4,930	9,700	600	700
5.	1,100	7,090	7,450	1,140
6.	4,600	3,900	5,100	600
7.	90	960	7,700	540
8.	300	720	150	800

Lesson 3.6, page 49

	a	b	c	d
1.	70	30	110	130
2.	140	170	260	250
3.	500	500	1100	800
4.	1,500	1,600	6,200	5,300
5.	5,000	13,000	12,000	5,000

Lesson 3.6, page 50
1. 900 2. 30 3. 800 4. 130 5. 500

Lesson 3.7, page 51

	a	b	c	d
1.	20	40	10	30
2.	380	930	730	480
3.	200	400	300	500
4.	800	2,400	4,100	7,000
5.	5,000	6,000	1,000	8,000

Lesson 3.7, page 52
1. 20 2. 100 3. 200 4. 110 5. 110

Posttest, page 53

	a	b	c	d	e
1.	63	89	153	102	189
2.	742	630	531	712	902
3.	6,293	6,348	9,256	6,553	7,974
4.	1,791	4,490	7,171	4,194	392
5.	6,506	3,192	2,882	2,891	1,884
6.	3,891	4,285	3,387	2,090	7,691
7.	600	90	400	980	

Posttest, page 54
8. 115 9. 1,894 10. 110 11. 1,000
12. 30

Grade 3 Answers

Mid-Test

page 55

	a	b	c	d	e
1.	8	19	35	26	26
2.	67	58	135	70	150
3.	139	140	719	1,008	1,113
4.	104	115	70	983	1,656
5.	40	26	7	8	16
6.	17	9	71	59	19
7.	480	114	513	541	711
8.	100	111	191	376	104

page 56

	a	b	c	d	e
9.	1,345	9,516	8,454	8,665	7,834
10.	9,093	7,372	6,963	4,512	8,993
11.	4,900	8,241	5,352	1,101	2,000
12.	4,786	6,990	2,091	7,881	4,891
13.	5,430	990	78,700	9,870	54,300
14.	8,400	500	400	270	1,800
15.	450	9,900	800	1,100	130
16.	7,700	2,400	380	740	800

page 57
17. 36 **18.** 72 **19.** 359 **20.** 33 **21.** 14
22. 7

page 58
23. 113 **24.** 80 **25.** 271 **26.** 956
27. 1,889 **28.** 20 **29.** 30

Chapter 4

Pretest, page 59

	a	b	c	d	e	f
1.	0	5	12	0	30	24
2.	14	27	64	18	20	20
3.	36	27	7	15	12	4

4.	0	28	54	16	5	18
5.	28	21	6	8	9	30
6.	80	30	60	90	80	80
7.	120	70	120	60	100	50
8.	160	30	140	120	180	180
9.	240	200	210	100	50	320

Pretest, page 60
10. 80 **11.** 60 **12.** 15 **13.** 60

Lesson 4.1, page 61

	a	b	c	d	e
1.	6	14	12	18	16
2.	4	2	15	18	9
3.	6	3	12	21	8
4.	16	4	20	36	32
5.	12	8	10	24	27
6.	24	28	6	21	18

Lesson 4.2, page 62

	a	b	c	d	e	f
1.	10	15	3	4	12	10
2.	0	1	15	4	0	12
3.	16	10	20	6	25	0
4.	8	0	9	16	6	2
5.	0	9	8	0	6	20
6.	5	0	3	25	0	8

Lesson 4.3, page 63
1. 4; 5; 20 **2.** 3; 2; 6 **3.** 4; 2; 8
4. Answers may vary—solution is 5
5. Answers may vary—solution is 12

Grade 3 Answers

Lesson 4.4, page 64

	a	b	c	d	e	f
1.	0	27	30	4	5	18
2.	18	40	40	0	18	12
3.	24	21	6	14	15	4
4.	12	25	9	8	21	0
5.	0	18	35	30	6	8
6.	28	9	9	14	0	3

Lesson 4.5, page 65

	a	b	c	d	e	f
1.	27	42	20	63	48	0
2.	12	40	36	0	35	18
3.	5	24	16	48	0	0
4.	3	24	18	12	18	30
5.	24	18	42	81	32	15
6.	12	64	27	28	0	49

Lesson 4.6, page 66

1. 6; 5; 30 2. 7; 9; 63
3. 4; 8; 32
4. Answers may vary—solution is 35
5. Answers may vary—solution is 36

Lesson 4.7, page 67

	a	b	c	d	e	f
1.	90	20	90	240	160	490
2.	200	400	540	80	400	480
3.	180	50	140	150	210	150
4.	80	30	360	630	120	250

Lesson 4.7, page 68

	a	b	c	d	e	f
1.	100	150	30	40	120	100
2.	150	40	180	40	210	120
3.	160	160	240	140	300	250
4.	320	0	350	360	60	80
5.	140	240	180	300	480	320
6.	450	630	30	450	0	160

7.	180	560	540	490	640	240
8.	350	810	270	360	560	210

Lesson 4.8, page 69

1. 60; 3; 180 2. 20; 4; 80
3. 30; 4; 120 4. 20 5. 60

Lesson 4.9, page 70

1. 84 2. 70 3. 25 4. 98

Posttest, page 71

	a	b	c	d	e	f
1.	5	81	6	20	18	0
2.	63	10	6	16	35	12
3.	30	24	12	0	12	28
4.	20	80	50	40	0	0
5.	100	80	30	60	100	60
6.	40	150	200	120	70	120
7.	210	300	120	160	150	90
8.	160	180	280	400	90	140
9.	120	180	40	150	90	400

Posttest, page 72

10. 20 11. 120 12. 150 13. 14 14. 80

Chapter 5

Pretest, page 73

	a	b	c	d	e
1.	9	9	2	2	6
2.	3	9	1	5	3
3.	2	7	8	8	4
4.	5	2	2	3	6
5.	7	7	8	7	8
6.	4	8	1	9	7
7.	5	3	5	6	6
8.	9	5	2	4	6
9.	1	4	4	5	8

Pretest, page 74

10. 9 11. 6 12. 8 13. 3 14. 2 15. 9

Grade 3 Answers

Lesson 5.1, page 75

1. 12; 2 **2.** 24; 3 **3.** 36; 9 **4.** 4; 8; 2
5. 7; 35; 5 **6.** 20; 4 **7.** 27; 3 **8.** 6; 3
9. 3; 15; 5 **10.** 2 ; 14 ; 7

Lesson 5.1, page 76

1a. 4; 4; $4 \times 3 = 12$
1b. 3; 3; $4 \times 3 = 12$
2a. 4; 5; 5; $5 \times 4 = 20$
2b. 5; 4; 4; $5 \times 4 = 20$
3a. 12; 2; 6; 6; $6 \times 2 = 12$
3b. 12; 6; 2; 2; $6 \times 2 = 12$

Lesson 5.2, page 77

1a. 2; $3 \times 2 = 6$ **1b.** 7; $2 \times 7 = 14$
1c. 5; $1 \times 5 = 5$ **1d.** 2; $2 \times 2 = 4$
1e. 4; $1 \times 4 = 4$ **2a.** 9; $3 \times 9 = 27$
2b. 3; $1 \times 3 = 3$ **2c.** 9; $2 \times 9 = 18$
2d. 7; $1 \times 7 = 7$ **2e.** 7; $3 \times 7 = 21$
3a. 4; $3 \times 4 = 12$ **3b.** 8; $2 \times 8 = 16$
3c. 5; $1 \times 5 = 5$ **3d.** 6; $3 \times 6 = 18$
3e. 5; $2 \times 5 = 10$ **4a.** 6; $1 \times 6 = 6$
4b. 8; $1 \times 8 = 8$ **4c.** 4; $2 \times 4 = 8$
4d. 2; $1 \times 2 = 2$ **4e.** 1; $1 \times 1 = 1$
5a. 8; $3 \times 8 = 24$ **5b.** 3; $3 \times 3 = 9$
5c. 9; $1 \times 9 = 9$ **5d.** 3; $2 \times 3 = 6$
5e. 1; $2 \times 1 = 2$

Lesson 5.2, page 78

1. 18; 3; 6 **2.** 16; 2; 8 **3.** 12; 2; 6
4. 5 **5.** 9

Lesson 5.3, page 79

1a. 9 ; $6 \times 9 = 54$ **1b.** 9 ; $3 \times 9 = 27$
1c. 8 ; $6 \times 8 = 48$ **1d.** 5 ; $5 \times 5 = 25$
1e. 9 ; $4 \times 9 = 36$ **2a.** 6 ; $5 \times 6 = 30$
2b. 6 ; $4 \times 6 = 24$ **2c.** 8 ; $4 \times 8 = 32$
2d. 4 ; $4 \times 4 = 16$ **2e.** 5 ; $4 \times 5 = 20$

	a	b	c	d	e
3.	6	7	7	4	7
4.	9	2	8	8	3
5.	4	8	3	9	3
6.	3	7	6	1	3

Lesson 5.3, page 80

1. 24; 6; 4 **2.** 30; 6; 5 **3.** 42; 6; 7
4. 3 **5.** 8

Lesson 5.4, page 81

1a. 1; $7 \times 1 = 7$ **1b.** 4; $6 \times 4 = 24$
1c. 7; $8 \times 7 = 56$ **1d.** 5; $6 \times 5 = 30$
1e. 8; $8 \times 8 = 64$ **2a.** 2; $6 \times 2 = 12$
2b. 5; $7 \times 5 = 35$ **2c.** 3; $8 \times 3 = 24$
2d. 4; $7 \times 4 = 28$ **2e.** 6; $6 \times 6 = 36$

	a	b	c	d	e
3.	7	9	8	7	3
4.	2	2	3	6	5
5.	7	2	3	1	6
6.	3	6	1	9	5

Lesson 5.4, page 82

1. 72; 9; 8 **2.** 40; 8; 5 **3.** 16; 8; 2 **4.** 9

Lesson 5.5, page 83

	a	b	c	d	e
1.	5	4	3	9	3
2.	9	9	8	7	1
3.	8	7	4	7	9
4.	2	2	5	3	3
5.	6	5	1	9	3
6.	4	9	4	6	9
7.	1	8	6	9	8
8.	6	5	7	6	5
9.	3	4	9	2	1
10.	7	7	1	2	7

Grade 3 Answers

Lesson 5.6, page 84

	a	b	c	d	e	f
1.	2	2	9	9	9	2
2.	5	6	3	3	8	4
3.	8	3	4	7	1	6
4.	6	2	9	1	4	5
5.	100	60	320	20	50	270
6.	42	300	400	90	280	80
7.	60	70	350	480	180	18
8.	400	280	140	160	200	270

Lesson 5.7, page 85

1. 6 2. 40 3. 11 4. 7

Posttest, page 86

	a	b	c	d	e
1.	4	8	7	6	4
2.	6	1	3	6	4
3.	2	5	6	2	2
4.	1	5	3	9	3
5.	7	5	3	5	6
6.	9	3	8	8	8
7.	9	4	4	6	4
8.	1	3	9	1	8
9.	7	7	6	8	7

Posttest, page 87

10. 8 11. 6 12. 5 13. 4 14. 9 15. 5

Chapter 6

Pretest, page 88

	a	b	c
1.	$\frac{2}{3}$	$\frac{1}{4}$	$\frac{1}{2}$
2.	$\frac{2}{4}$ or $\frac{1}{2}$	$\frac{6}{8}$ or $\frac{3}{4}$	$\frac{5}{8}$
3.	$\frac{1}{2}$	$\frac{1}{4}$	$\frac{3}{4}$

4. number line: 0, $\frac{1}{6}$, $\frac{4}{6}$, 1

Pretest, page 89

	a	b	c
5.	$\frac{1}{2} > \frac{1}{4}$	$\frac{2}{3} < \frac{3}{4}$	$\frac{1}{4} < \frac{1}{3}$
6.	$\frac{3}{4} > \frac{1}{2}$	$\frac{1}{2} > \frac{1}{3}$	$\frac{1}{2} = \frac{2}{4}$

7. number line: 0, $\frac{3}{8}$, $1 = \frac{8}{8}$

8. $\frac{6}{6}$, 1

Lesson 6.1, page 90

	a	b	c
1.	$\frac{1}{3}$	$\frac{3}{4}$	$\frac{4}{5}$
2.	$\frac{1}{10}$	$\frac{3}{8}$	$\frac{1}{2}$
3.	$\frac{2}{3}$	$\frac{4}{8}$ or $\frac{1}{2}$	$\frac{2}{5}$
4.	$\frac{2}{4}$ or $\frac{1}{2}$	$\frac{3}{5}$	$\frac{4}{10}$ or $\frac{2}{5}$

Lesson 6.2, page 91

	a	b	c
1.	$\frac{4}{5}$	$\frac{1}{4}$	$\frac{4}{8}$
2.	$\frac{1}{10}$	$\frac{2}{3}$	$\frac{3}{8}$
3.	$\frac{1}{2}$	$\frac{2}{5}$	$\frac{9}{10}$

	a	b	c	d

Placement of shaded pieces may vary.

4.

Lesson 6.3, page 92

	a	b	c
1.	$\frac{1}{4} < \frac{3}{4}$	$\frac{1}{2} = \frac{2}{4}$	$\frac{2}{3} > \frac{1}{2}$
2.	$\frac{7}{10} > \frac{3}{5}$	$\frac{3}{8} < \frac{3}{4}$	$\frac{1}{3} < \frac{5}{8}$
3.	$\frac{1}{5} = \frac{2}{10}$	$\frac{3}{4} > \frac{1}{2}$	$\frac{6}{10} > \frac{2}{5}$

Lesson 6.3, page 93

	a	b	c
1.	$\frac{1}{2} = \frac{2}{4}$	$\frac{2}{3} < \frac{3}{4}$	$\frac{1}{5} < \frac{2}{5}$
2.	$\frac{3}{4} < \frac{7}{8}$	$\frac{2}{3} > \frac{1}{4}$	$\frac{5}{8} < \frac{2}{3}$
3.	$\frac{4}{5} = \frac{8}{10}$	$\frac{1}{2} < \frac{3}{4}$	$\frac{5}{8} < \frac{8}{10}$

Answer Key

Grade 3 Answers

Lesson 6.4, page 94

1. number line: 0, $\frac{1}{4}$, 1

2. number line: 0, $\frac{3}{4}$, 1

3. number line: 0, $\frac{1}{3}$, 1

4. number line: 0, $\frac{2}{3}$, 1

5. number line: 0, $1 = \frac{4}{4}$

Lesson 6.5, page 95

1. no; $\frac{2}{8}$ and $\frac{1}{4}$ or $\frac{4}{8}$ and $\frac{2}{4}$ or $\frac{6}{8}$ and $\frac{3}{4}$

2. no; $\frac{1}{3}$ and $\frac{2}{6}$ or $\frac{2}{3}$ and $\frac{4}{6}$

Lesson 6.6, page 96

1. $\frac{4}{4}=1$ 2. $\frac{3}{3}=1$ 3. $\frac{2}{2}=1$ 4. $\frac{5}{5}=1$ 5. $\frac{10}{10}=1$ 6. $\frac{8}{8}=1$

Posttest, page 97

	a	b	c
1.	$\frac{1}{5}$	$\frac{3}{4}$	$\frac{1}{3}$
2.	$\frac{1}{4}$	$\frac{3}{5}$	$\frac{1}{2}$

3. number line: 0, $\frac{1}{4}$, $\frac{3}{4}$, 1

4. number line: 0, $\frac{3}{8}$, $\frac{5}{8}$, 1

Posttest, page 98

	a	b	c
5.	$\frac{1}{5}<\frac{2}{5}$	$\frac{1}{3}<\frac{7}{8}$	$\frac{4}{8}=\frac{1}{2}$
6.	$\frac{1}{2}<\frac{3}{4}$	$\frac{1}{4}>\frac{1}{8}$	$\frac{2}{3}<\frac{6}{8}$

7. number line: 0, $\frac{1}{3}$, $1 = \frac{3}{3}$

8. $\frac{4}{4}$, 1

Chapter 7

Pretest, page 99

	a	b
1.	c	a

2. 120 g

3a.
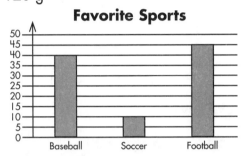

Favorite Sports

3b.

3rd Graders' Bedtimes	
8:00	● ●
8:30	●
9:00	● ● ● ●

Key ___●___ = 4

Pretest, page 100

	a	b
4.	12	12

5. 7 × 4 grid: 4 ... 4, 7, 7 → 28

6. 18 7. 48 8. 216

Lesson 7.1, page 101

1. 90 kilograms 2. 500 liters
3. 5,000 grams 4. 1 gram 5. 46
6. 2 7. 7 8. 10

Grade 3 Answers

Lesson 7.1, page 102

1. 1,000 liters **2.** 1 gram **3.** 2 liters
4. 700 grams **5.** 36 **6.** 100 **7.** 24 **8.** 5

Lesson 7.2, page 103

Flowers In My Garden

Daisies	🌸🌸 🌸🌸 🌸🌸 🌸🌸
Roses	🌸🌸 🌸🌸 🌸
Sunflowers	🌸🌸

Key: 🌸🌸 = 2 flowers

15 total flowers

Lesson 7.3, page 104

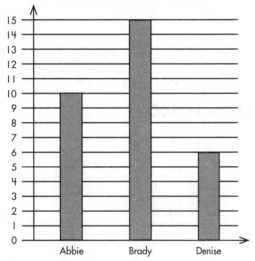

Candle Sale Totals

9 more candles

Lesson 7.4, page 105

1. $3\frac{3}{4}$ **2.** 4 **3.** $4\frac{1}{2}$ **4.** 4 **5.** $4\frac{1}{2}$
6. $4\frac{1}{2}$ **7.** $3\frac{3}{4}$ **8.** $4\frac{1}{2}$ **9.** $3\frac{3}{4}$

10.

Crayons Used in the Classroom (in.)

Lesson 7.4, page 106

1. $1\frac{3}{4}$ **2.** $2\frac{1}{2}$ **3.** $1\frac{3}{4}$ **4.** $1\frac{1}{2}$ **5.** $1\frac{1}{2}$
6. $1\frac{3}{4}$ **7.** $2\frac{1}{2}$

8.

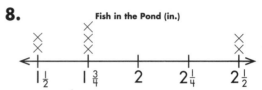

Fish in the Pond (in.)

Lesson 7.5, page 107

1. 12 **2.** 10 **3.** 24 **4.** 28 **5.** 7 **6.** 12

Lesson 7.5, page 108

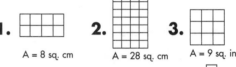

1. A = 8 sq. cm **2.** A = 28 sq. cm **3.** A = 9 sq. in.
4. A = 3 sq. m **5.** A = 4 sq. cm **6.** A = 5 sq. cm

Lesson 7.6, page 109

	a	b	c	d
1.	50	56	40	300
2.	126	40	160	160

Lesson 7.6, page 110

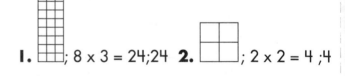

1. ; 8 × 3 = 24; 24 **2.** ; 2 × 2 = 4 ; 4
3. ; 1 × 4 = 4; 4
4. ; 3 × 9 = 27; 27

Lesson 7.7, page 111

1. Drawings may vary; 25
2. Drawings may vary; 41
3. Drawings may vary; 24

Grade 3 Answers

Lesson 7.8, page 112
1. 80 2. 90 3. 450 4. 81 5. 810
6. 56 7. 90

Lesson 7.9, page 113

	a	b	c
1.	14	30	28
2.	225	120	55
3.	5	8	30

Lesson 7.9, page 114
1. 25 2. 100 3. 52 4. 306 5. 192
6. 36 7. 40

Posttest, page 115

	a	b
1.	a	b
2.	8	

3a.

Miles Canoed	
Team #1	X X X
Team #2	X X
Team #3	X X X X X X X

Key ___X___ = 20

3b.
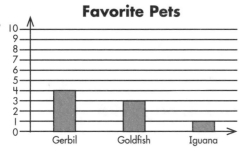
Favorite Pets

Posttest, page 116

	a	b
4.	6	9

5. ; 24

---

6. 12 7. 33 8. 27cm

Chapter 8

Pretest, page 117

	a	b	c	d
1.	32; 2	28; 3		
2.	45; 3	15; 4		
3.	50; 9	10; 10		
4.	2:00	1:30	1:45	1:43
5.	7:45	1:30		

6.

5 hours

Lesson 8.1, page 118

	a	b	c	d
1.	15; 6	10; 12		
2.	50; 7	10; 8		
3.	45; 12	15; 1		
4.	30; 1	30; 2		
5.	4:20	6:13	7:10	1:50
6.	6:45	8:09	12:30	2:23

Lesson 8.1, page 119

	a	b	c	d
1.	2:00	2:30	2:15	2:20
2.	9:00	8:30	8:30	8:36

	a	b
3.		
4.		

Grade 3 Answers

Lesson 8.2, page 120

1.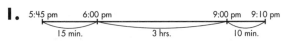

5:45 pm — 6:00 pm — 9:00 pm — 9:10 pm
15 min. — 3 hrs. — 10 min.

3 hours, 25 minutes

2.

7:45 am — 8:00 am — 4:00 pm — 4:15 pm
15 min. — 8 hrs. — 15 min.

8 hours, 30 minutes

Posttest, page 121

	a	b	c	d
1.	15; 4	45; 5		
2.	55; 12	5; 1		
3.	40; 6	20; 7		
4.	7:00	7:30	7:15	7:19

5.

8:40 am — 9:00am — 12:00pm — 12:10 pm
20 min. — 3 hrs. — 10 min.

3 hours, 30 minutes

6.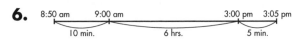

8:50 am — 9:00 am — 3:00 pm — 3:05 pm
10 min. — 6 hrs. — 5 min.

6 hours, 15 minutes

Chapter 9

Pretest, page 122

1.

$\frac{1}{4}$ $\frac{1}{4}$
$\frac{1}{4}$ $\frac{1}{4}$

2.

$\frac{1}{3}$ $\frac{1}{3}$ $\frac{1}{3}$

3.

$\frac{1}{6}$ $\frac{1}{6}$ $\frac{1}{6}$ $\frac{1}{6}$ $\frac{1}{6}$ Answers may vary.

4. 4; 4; 0 **5.** 0; 0 ;0 **6.** 4; 4; 0
7. 6; 0; 0; 12 **8.** 1; 4; 0; 8 **9.** 0; 0; 0; 0

10. ◇ ▽ ▱ ▱
11. □ □ □
12. □ ▱ ◇ ◇

Lesson 9.1, page 123

	a	b	c	d	
1.	△	▭	□	○	

	a	b	c	d	e
2.	0	4	3	4	3
3.	0	4	1	4	0
4.	0	0	2	0	3

Lesson 9.2, page 124

1. 6; 0; 0 **2.** 0; 6; 0 **3.** 1; 0; 4 **4.** 0
5. 8 **6.** 12 **7.** 12 **8.** 5 **9.** Answers may vary.
10. Answers may vary.

Lesson 9.3, page 125

1. □ ◇ ▽ ▱
2. □ ◇ ▱
3. □ □ ◇ □
4. ▱ □ ◇ ◇
5. □ ◇
6. square

Lesson 9.4, page 126

Shape divisions may vary.

1. $\frac{1}{2}$ $\frac{1}{2}$

2. $\frac{1}{3}$ $\frac{1}{3}$ $\frac{1}{3}$

Grade 3 Answers

3.

4.

5.

6.   Shape divisions may vary.

7.

8.

Posttest, page 127

	a	b
1.		
2.		

	a	b	c	d
3a.	rectangle, quadrilateral, or parallelogram			
3b.	quadrilateral, rhombus, or parallelogram			
3c.	parallelogram, quadrilateral, rectangle, rhombus, or square			
3d.	quadrilateral			
4.	4	12	4	8

Chapter 10

Pretest, page 128

	a	b	c	d
1.	18	14	10	6
2.	4	5	6,	7
3.	20	25	30	35
4.	32	64	128	256
5.	7	9	11	13
6.	7	6	5	4

7. $36 \div \square = 6$; 6   **8.** $5 \times 4 = \square$; 20

9. $\square \div 3 = 7$; 21   **10.** $\square \times 4 = 24$; 6

11. $35 \div 5 = \square$; 7   **12.** $9 \times \square = 18$; 2

13. $\square \div 3 = 6$; 18

Pretest, page 129

	a	b	c	d
14.	0	5	7	6
15.	7	5	3	2
16.	30; 30	48; 48	10; 10	
17.	7; 2	48; 48		

17c. $2 \times 4 = 8$; $8 \times 5 = 40$; 40

18. 4; 20; 8; 28

19. 7; 60; 42; 102

20. 5; 70; 35; 105

Lesson 10.1, page 130

	a	b	c
1.	8	10	12
2.	7	9	11
3.	14	12	10
4.	6	3	1
5.	10	9	8
6.	20	25	30
7.	12	15	18

Grade 3 Answers

8.	110	160	220
9.	7	4	1
10.	7	6	5

Lesson 10.2, page 131

	a	b	c	d
1.	4	6	0	0
2.	2	5	1	1
3.	2	4	1	4
4.	5	3	5	4
5.	4	6	2	5
6.	5	5	2	6
7.	3	6	2	3

Lesson 10.2, page 132

1a. $2 \times 3 = 6$; $6 \times 5 = 30$; d = 30
1b. $1 \times 2 = 2$; $2 \times 9 = 18$; h = 18
2a. $2 \times 4 = 8$; $8 \times 6 = 48$; e = 48
2b. $2 \times 4 = 8$; $8 \times 7 = 56$; g = 56
3a. 2; 40 + 8; 48
3b. 4; 30 + 12; 42
4a. 9; 20 + 18; 38
4b. 6; 50 + 30; 80

Lesson 10.2, page 133

1. $2 + 3 = \square$; five **2.** $7 - 2 = \square$; five
3. $4 \times 3 = \square$; twelve **4.** $14 \div 2 = \square$; seven
5. $\square + 5 = 7$; two **6.** $13 - \square = 10$; three

Lesson 10.2, page 134

1. $27 \div \square = 3$; 9 **2.** $\square \div 8 = 8$; 64
3. $12 \div 3 = \square$; 4 **4.** $4 \times 9 = \square$; 36
5. $\square \times 8 = 56$; 7 **6.** $9 \times \square = 81$; 9
7. $20 \div 4 = \square$; 5 **8.** $10 \times \square = 90$; 9
9. $\square \times 5 = 25$; 5 **10.** $\square \div 7 = 9$; 63

Posttest, page 135

	a	b	c	d
1.	4	5	6	7
2.	35	30	25	20
3.	70	60	50	40
4.	16	20	24	28
5.	8	10	12	14
6.	39	41	43	45

7. $12 \div 6 = \square$; 2 **8.** $7 \times 3 = \square$; 21
9. $5 + 6 = \square$; 11 **10.** $\square \div 4 = 8$; 32
11. $9 \times \square = 72$; 8 **12.** $12 \times 5 = \square$; 60

Posttest, page 136

	a	b	c	d
13.	0	4	2	3
14.	3	6	6	3

15a. 18; 18 **15b.** 8; 8 **15c.** 36; 36
16a. $2 \times 3 = 6$; $6 \times 8 = 48$; a = 48
16b. $1 \times 2 = 2$; $2 \times 7 = 14$; c = 14
16c. $5 \times 1 = 5$; $5 \times 6 = 30$; k = 30
17. 3; 70 + 21 = 91
18. 6; 60 + 36 = 96
19. 8; 40 + 32 = 72

Final Test

page 137

	a	b	c	d	e
1.	13	22	63	96	61
2.	494	264	179	1,310	820
3.	12	35	293	499	398
4.	21	41	1	14	490
5.	6,244	7,068	1,503	8,464	4,057
6.	3,830	4,071	2,583	4,932	3,039

Grade 3 Answers

7. 1881 **8.** 24

Page 138

	a	b	c	d	e
9.	4,930	7,300	600	700	
10.	12	250	120	56	120
11.	150	90	50	20	180
12.	8	4	6	3	1
13.	3	5	2	3	5

14. 140 **15.** 8

Page 139

	a	b	c	d
16.	$\frac{3}{4}$	$\frac{1}{2}$	$\frac{5}{8}$	$\frac{1}{8}$
17.	$\frac{1}{2} < \frac{3}{4}$	$\frac{1}{2} = \frac{2}{4}$	$\frac{1}{3} < \frac{1}{2}$	
18.	$\frac{2}{3} < \frac{3}{4}$	$\frac{3}{4} > \frac{4}{8}$	$\frac{1}{2} = \frac{3}{6}$	

19.

```
<---+-------+-------+---->
    0              3/4  1
```

20.

```
<---+-------+-------+---->
    0          2/3     1
```

21. $\frac{4}{4}=1$ **22.** $\frac{3}{3}=1$

Page 140

	a	b
23.	b	b
24.	22	

	a	b	c
25.	9	14	18
26.	60		

Page 141

27.

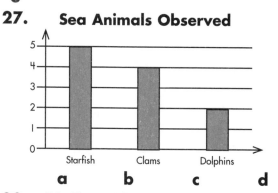

Sea Animals Observed

	a	b	c	d
28.	42; 7	18; 8		
29.	3:00	3:30	3:15	3:16

30. 11 **31.** 8 **32.** dog **33.** rabbit

Page 142

34a. circle; polygon **34b.** sphere; solid
 34c. rectangular prism; solid

34d. cylinder; solid **35a.** quadrilateral

35b. quadrilateral, square, rectangle, parallelogram, or rhombus

35c. quadrilateral, parallelogram, or rectangle

35d. quadrilateral, parallelogram, or rhombus

36a. (circle divided into $\frac{1}{2}$ and $\frac{1}{2}$)

36b. (rectangle divided into $\frac{1}{4}$ $\frac{1}{4}$ $\frac{1}{4}$ $\frac{1}{4}$) Shape divisions may vary.

36c.  (triangle divided into $\frac{1}{3}$ $\frac{1}{3}$ $\frac{1}{3}$)

	a	b	c	d
37.	35	40	7	5
38.	3	5	3	7

39. $5 \times 2 = \square$; 10

Notes

 Sometimes when you try to divide a number into equal groups, part of the number is left over. This is called the **remainder**. Use these steps to find the remainder.

1.
$$5 \overline{)16}$$

Think: 5 x __ is the closest to 16?

2.
$$\begin{array}{r} 3 \\ 5 \overline{)16} \\ -15 \\ \hline 1 \end{array}$$

3.
$$\begin{array}{r} 3\ R\ 1 \\ 5 \overline{)16} \\ -15 \\ \hline 1 \end{array}$$

There are 5 groups of 3 with 1 left over.

Divide.

A.
$$\begin{array}{r} 1\ R4 \\ 6 \overline{)10} \\ -6 \\ \hline 4 \end{array}$$

$$2 \overline{)9}$$

B.
$$3 \overline{)20}$$
$$2 \overline{)19}$$
$$6 \overline{)47}$$
$$6 \overline{)41}$$

C.
$$7 \overline{)51}$$
$$2 \overline{)15}$$
$$3 \overline{)22}$$
$$7 \overline{)48}$$

D.
$$2 \overline{)11}$$
$$4 \overline{)26}$$
$$6 \overline{)19}$$
$$5 \overline{)27}$$

 **Louie jumps hurdles for his track meet. He jumps the same number in each race. In his last 6 races, he jumped 36 hurdles. How many hurdles did he jump each day?**

Scholastic

dividing with remainders

Divide.

A. 5)‾41‾   6)‾52‾   3)‾19‾   8)‾74‾

(handwritten for A: 8 r1, 40, 1)

B. 4)‾29‾   2)‾13‾   7)‾38‾   9)‾46‾

C. 5)‾21‾   6)‾31‾   3)‾26‾   8)‾57‾

D. 4)‾14‾   2)‾7‾   7)‾65‾   9)‾51‾

E. 3)‾13‾   6)‾39‾   5)‾14‾   8)‾50‾

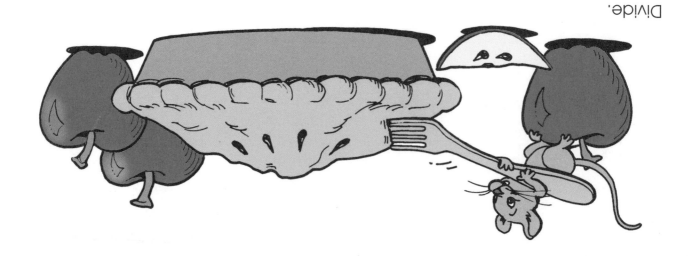

Candy's mom bought 56 apples to make 8 pies. If she used an equal number of apples in each pie, how many apples did she use in each pie? Solve on another piece of paper.

dividing without remainders—
2-digit dividends

 Remember to follow each step when dividing larger numbers.

1. Divide the tens digit by the divisor. Multiply. Subtract.

$$3\overline{)45}$$
$$\frac{-3}{1}$$

2. Bring down the ones digit. Divide this number by the divisor.

$$3\overline{)45}$$
$$\frac{-3}{15}\!\uparrow$$

3. Multiply. Subtract.

$$3\overline{)45}$$
$$\frac{-3}{15}\!\uparrow$$
$$\frac{-15}{0}$$

Divide.

A. $2\overline{)58}$ $\qquad$ $5\overline{)85}$ $\qquad$ $6\overline{)72}$ $\qquad$ $5\overline{)90}$

B. $3\overline{)48}$ $\qquad$ $8\overline{)96}$ $\qquad$ $2\overline{)74}$ $\qquad$ $4\overline{)92}$

C. $6\overline{)78}$ $\qquad$ $4\overline{)76}$ $\qquad$ $5\overline{)65}$ $\qquad$ $4\overline{)60}$

 Andrew has 87 marbles. He divides them into 3 bags. How many marbles are in each bag? Solve. Then circle the problem above with the same quotient.

Scholastic

finding missing dividends

At our family reunion picnic, 8 people sat at each picnic table. We needed 16 tables. How many people altogether were at the reunion?

Are we missing?

Write each missing dividend.

A. ___ ÷ 9 = 7   ___ ÷ 4 = 6   ___ ÷ 6 = 6   ___ ÷ 5 = 7

B. ___ ÷ 3 = 3   ___ ÷ 2 = 9   ___ ÷ 8 = 6   ___ ÷ 9 = 9

C. ___ ÷ 4 = 8   ___ ÷ 3 = 7   ___ ÷ 2 = 8   ___ ÷ 6 = 3

D. ___ ÷ 8 = 8   ___ ÷ 1 = 9   ___ ÷ 5 = 6   ___ ÷ 7 = 1

E. ___ ÷ 4 = 40   ___ ÷ 3 = 30   ___ ÷ 3 = 100

F. ___ ÷ 7 = 60   ___ ÷ 5 = 60   ___ ÷ 2 = 40

Remember that multiplication and division are related. Multiplying the quotient by the divisor will tell you the dividend.

Hi! Aren't we related?

You bet! When you multiply us, our missing product is the missing dividend!